AF593645

HONDA

HONDA

HONDA

Edited by
Mick Woollett

TEMPLE PRESS

TEMPLE · PRESS

NEWNES·BOOKS

Published by Temple Press
an imprint of Newnes Books
84/88 The Centre, Feltham, Middlesex, TW13 4BH, England
and distributed for them by
The Hamlyn Publishing Group Limited
Rushden, Northants, England

The publishers wish to thank Honda (U.K.) Limited for their help and advice in the preparation of this book.

First published 1983

ISBN 0 600 34994 2

Printed in Italy

Contents

Introduction

Honda motor cycles are now such an integral part of the Western way of life that it is difficult to believe that machines bearing the now famous name were first launched on the world market only a little over 20 years ago . . . and that exports in numbers started as recently as 1965.

Since then Honda machines have penetrated virtually every market in the Western world and exports have climbed from 37,000 in 1960 to a staggering 2 million plus in 1982.

These figures are all the more remarkable because the Honda sales drive started at a time when the post-war two-wheeler boom in Europe had died. In fact several of the famous European manufacturers had foundered before a single Honda had been sold in Europe – the famous Vincent works in Stevenage shut up shop in the mid-1950s, Norton had been forced to amalgamate with AJS and Matchless to keep going, while NSU of Germany had switched production from two-wheelers to cars.

Honda, followed by the other Japanese makers, went out and, using modern sales methods, created a brand new market – one which initially helped to keep the ailing European and American manufacturers going rather than destroying them.

Remarkably the incredible Honda success story was achieved mainly thanks to the romantic dream of a very unorthodox Japanese, Soichiro Honda. Son of a blacksmith, a thoroughly practical engineer with little formal education, Soichiro Honda pursued his dream to build better motor cycles and to sell them around the world with a restless energy that overcame thousands of problems along the way.

He realised five years before he began to market his machines in Europe that the fastest and most effective way to break down sales resistance to Japanese machines was through success on the racing circuits of the world.

How Honda went about this is the subject of two chapters of this book, and it is interesting to note that he also fully understood the importance of success to the workers at Honda. How producing winning machines would lift their morale and help them to perform their often boring, routine assembly line work with pride and satisfaction. He also understood the importance of continual research and development to create new and exciting models to stimulate the market.

The success of his venture has been spectacular. Statistics can be dull but when you consider that Honda production now tops 3 million machines a year and that the total number of motor cycles and mopeds built by Honda topped the 45 million mark in mid-1983 you begin to grasp the scope of the project that started with one man's dream and a single basic model in the late 1940s.

Mick Woollett

Soichiro Honda- the Man and his Machines

The Honda Motor Company was started, like every other motor cycle company, with one man and his dream. The man was Soichiro Honda and his dream was to build motor cycles for the masses. He was so successful in what he did that within 20 years Honda had become established as the world's biggest manufacturer of motor cycles, a position it still holds today. Because the Honda of the 1980s is so large, it is a salutary exercise to look back at the rise and rise of Soichiro Honda and the skyrocketing growth of the firm he founded in 1946.

Honda's origins are humble enough. He was born in 1906, the eldest son of the blacksmith in the tiny village of Komyo, long since engulfed by modern-day Hamamatsu. The young Honda developed an interest in machinery long before he started school and would often sit for hours in the local rice-polishing mill watching the noisy, smelly stationary petrol engine they used to power the machinery.

At school he was hardly a model student. He had a scant regard for pure book learning, preferring instead the practical approach. Even today his company does not operate the rigid hierarchical promotional structure that determines advancement by educational achievement.

The man who started it all – Soichiro Honda

Honda finished just eight years of formal education and graduated from school in 1922, aged 16. He took up an apprenticeship in Tokyo to learn the car trade and within a few years returned to Hamamatsu to open a garage of his own. The business took off and by the time he was 25 years old Honda's garage was making profits of 1,000 yen a month – a grand amount for the 1930s.

That kind of success was hardly typical, especially in pre-war Japan where success and wealth were supposed to come with age. But then there is nothing typical about Honda. When he began to earn a lot of money, he decided he would use his new-found wealth to have a great time, rapidly gaining a reputation as a bit of a playboy – definitely *not* the done thing in pre-war Japan. He has also never held the traditional Japanese view that convention and respect for authority in all its forms are paramount. A real maverick, he has always been controversial.

An illustration of this is an extraordinary scene which happened whilst Honda was still running his car repair business. It seems that he had had a disagreement with the local income tax office. Unable to bring them round to his way of thinking by conventional tactics, Honda tried the unconventional: he hired a fire engine at great expense, drove down to the office and waited for the workers to emerge on their way home. When they came out of the door Honda aimed his fire hose at them and soaked the lot!

Honda's successful business allowed him to indulge another of his pleasures – racing. He built his own speedboat and a massively powerful car using a surplus American Curtiss Wright aero engine. Honda won several races but finally gave up competition after a 100 mph (160 kph) crash in 1936. He was leading the All-Japan Speed Rally in his modified Ford racer when a car suddenly pulled across his path. Honda was badly hurt in the crash but 18 months later he was back at work.

Ever ambitious Honda decided that manufacturing would be more lucrative than his repair business. At the age of 30 he announced that he was going to start making piston rings, reasoning that they were a commodity that would always be in demand. But he had not reckoned on the technology necessary to make reliable rings. His first efforts were a disaster, but with 50 men hired, a factory bought and cash borrowed he had to persevere.

This was a difficult time for Honda. He ran down his savings whilst trying to find a formula, and it was months before he hit upon a suitable metal mix. That was only after a local university professor analysed one of Honda's early efforts and pointed out that it lacked silicone.

Finally, late in November 1937, Honda's new firm (he called it Tokai Seiki Heavy Industries) produced their first acceptable piston rings.

However, the whole experience was salutary for the young Honda. He admitted to the professor that he did not even know what silicone was, never mind that it was a necessary constituent of piston rings. It worried Honda so much that he enrolled himself in the Hamamatsu Institute of Technology to learn about metallurgy.

Honda adopted a cavalier attitude to study at the Institute: he only attended the lectures he decided were worthwhile so he was not surprised when after two years the principal, Tei Adachi, called him into his office and explained that he could not be awarded a diploma. But Honda was unrepentant: 'The diploma? That's worth less than a cinema ticket,' he told the astonished professor. 'The ticket guarantees that you can get into the cinema, but the diploma can't guarantee that you can make a living.'

Honda's piston rings were supplied all over Japan and as the pool of male labour dried up because of the Second World War he developed a sophisticated machine to produce them that could be operated by unskilled women. As his business expanded he even took on the job of manufacturing wooden aircraft propellors for the Japanese Air Force. His ingenuity came into play here too: he designed a machine that could automatically plane the complex curves of the propellor and produce them at a previously unheard of rate.

Tokai Seiki was bombed heavily by the Americans towards the end of the war, and in January 1945 was completely destroyed by an earthquake. The final surrender of Japan came as Honda and his men were trying to repair the machinery.

With the war over and an uncertain future ahead of him, Honda sold Tokai Seiki to Toyota, who he had been supplying with piston rings and decided to keep a low profile for a year. Rather like the hippies of the 1960s, Honda 'dropped out'. He went on drinking sessions, he threw parties and spent a lot of time playing the shakuhachi – a bamboo flute.

However, he kept looking for a business he could turn his hand to for he still had enough savings to start up again. Finally, almost as a stop-gap measure, he established the Honda Technical Research Institute in a tiny wooden shack 18 × 12 feet (5.53 × 3.6 m) on a levelled bomb site in downtown Hamamatsu. It was October 1946.

The Hamamatsu branch of the ART car repair business, started in 1946 by Soichiro Honda, was the forerunner of The Honda Motor Company of today

Post-war Japan was in a terrible shape: the economy was bankrupt and industry had collapsed. One of the biggest problems was transport: what little there was was chaotic and overcrowded, and that is what first turned Honda's mind to bikes. He hated being jammed in trains and the petrol rationing and extreme shortage meant that he could not use his car. As luck would have it he came across a job lot of 500 war surplus petrol engines that had been used by the military for generators. Honda, with his genius of improvisation, decided that these little motors would be just the thing to power a push-bike and within weeks he was selling complete machines.

The bikes were a success – his dozen or so workers could turn out one a day with ease and customers came from all over Japan to buy them. Inevitably the 500 motors were soon used up. Honda decided that the business was much too promising to give up so he immediately set himself to designing and building a petrol engine of his own.

Honda attracted a certain amount of criticism for his bike project – some people said he should not be building motor bikes with the petrol crisis and some said that his bikes were only being used by black marketeers to peddle their wares. He countered this by pointing out that not only did his machines economise on fuel they also could be used by starving city dwellers searching the countryside for food.

Actually many people ran the early Hondas on a turpentine and petrol mixture – a fuel that Honda himself produced. He extracted turpentine from the roots of pine trees in a forest he bought jointly with his father and used the oil to eke out the petrol he bought on the black market. The mixture was not very efficient – often up to 15 minutes' frantic pedalling was necessary before the engine would warm up enough to get underway and the exhaust emitted a smokey stench of turps. Thus Honda's customers were able to insist that they were not violating any petrol controls: 'Why you can smell that I'm using turpentine,' they would protest.

Honda's first own-brand engine was modelled on the old surplus motors and was unkindly dubbed the 'chimney', probably because of its turpentine-smokey exhaust. The 'chimney' was a 0.5 hp 50 cc two-stroke motor officially known as the A-type. Orders flooded in and things progressed so fast that in September 1948, less than two years after he founded the Technical Research Institute, the Honda Motor Company was founded.

Honda's A-type was developed into the 90 cc B-type in 1948, but Honda was working flat out to produce a new, more powerful machine that, he had decided, would use a frame of his own design. The first prototype was completed in August 1949. It was an air-cooled two-stroke (as all the Hondas had been so far) and had a displacement of 98 cc. Power output was a respectable 3 bhp and it had a two-speed gearbox. But the machine's most interesting feature was the frame. This was a pressed steel affair of immense strength. After the new machine had completed successful road trials, Honda and his workforce of 20 men sat down and toasted their success in doburoku – rough, strong saki. They had to give the bike a name, as clearly a letter on its own was not good enough. All fell silent as they contemplated their success. Suddenly one shouted: 'This is like a dream'. 'That's it!' exclaimed Honda. 'We shall call it the Dream.'

It was in October 1949 that a man who was set to become Honda's 'alter ego' and mastermind the company's international expansion joined the team. He was Takeo Fujisawa, a marketing genius Honda had met two months earlier on a visit to Tokyo to find an investor.

Fujisawa joined Honda just in time. The Japanese economy was slipping into recession and many of Honda's outlets, mostly small bicycle shops, were going bust; those that were not found it hard to make payments.

Fujisawa's first task was to sort out the rather 'ad hoc' distribution arrangement Honda had built up. Perhaps because Honda had always supplied them with engines on their own he saw no reason to do things differently now that he was producing a complete motor cycle. In fact he fully supported another company who were manufacturing a tubular frame for the Dream.

Kiyoshi Kawashima who has been with Honda since graduating from college in 1948 is now President of the Honda Motor Company

The dealers, then, were receiving first the old A-type motor for fitment to push-bike frames, the Dream motor which they could fit into the rival frame *and* the complete Dream itself. The situation was aggravated by the fact that the Dream with the rival frame was proving more popular than the Dream itself, despite the fact that the latter proved less prone to breakages over Japan's potholed streets. Fujisawa sorted the business out by insisting that dealers choose Honda or the rival frame company because they were now not allowed to sell both machines.

Sales of the Dream were good, but not good enough, so Fujisawa urged Honda to develop a new machine. He was not a technical man, but he told Honda that what was wanted was a four-stroke machine: 'Our two-strokes make an unpleasant high-pitched noise,' he said. 'The four-strokes have pleasant sounds, that's why ours are not selling.'

With Fujisawa named Director in Charge of Sales in 1950 Honda opened an office in Tokyo – the key to their big-time expansion. Pre-war Osaka had been Japan's commercial centre, but Tokyo was emerging as the hub of the new business community. When Fujisawa had earlier told Honda that a four-stroke motor would be the key to really big sales, the reply he got went something like: 'Oh, well all those other four-strokes are no good.'

But Honda the engineer and innovator was always driven onward to develop new machinery and, within months of that conversation with Fujisawa, Honda and Kiyoshi Kawashima (a bright young engineer recruited from the Hamamatsu Institute of Technology in 1948) had designed a four-stroke single-cylinder motor with overhead valves that displaced 146 cc. The first drawings were made in May 1951 and initial tests of the prototype Type E Dream were made in July.

The first tests on 15 July were an instant success. With Kawashima as test rider and Honda and Fujisawa following in a car the team set off for the mountainous area of Hakone. Kawashima and the new Dream made it to the top of the pass well ahead of Honda and Fujisawa. The bike had recorded an average speed of 43 mph (69 kph) up a pass that most of the contemporary side-valve-engined machines could scarcely manage without several stops to cool down. In recognition of his contribution to the new Dream Type E, Kawashima was made a director of Honda at the age of 34.

Using Fujisawa's massively expanded and now national dealer network, production of Hondas was greatly increased at the new plant, built at Kami-jujo to the north of Tokyo. The Dream Type D was being built at a rate of 300 units a month by late 1950, but the Type E soon eclipsed it. In fact in 1953 no fewer than 32,000 were produced.

Although the new Dream was successful (the

Dream type Ds on the Tokyo plant assembly line in 1951

Tokyo plant had switched early on to producing only the new machine), Honda and Fujisawa both came to the same conclusion that in their rush to produce a technically excellent and sophisticated piece of machinery they had neglected the real mass market that Honda had first tapped five years earlier with his motorised bicycles.

Within a year Honda had such a motor cycle. Known as the F-Type Cub, the red and white 'auto bai' had a 50 cc two-stroke engine which was designed to clip onto the rear end of any bicycle (it could be bought separately). The new machine was an instant success. Production at the old Hamamatsu plant was given over almost entirely to the Cub, and in recognition of its success, Honda was given the Blue Ribbon medal in the Emperor's New Year's Day Honours list in 1952. By the end of 1952, sales of the Cub had reached nearly 6,500 a month and accounted for almost three-quarters of all Japan's production of clip-on units.

That same year the Dreams were exported out East to Okinawa and the Philippines while a new plant at Shirako, near Tokyo, was established.

Ambitious as he was, Honda in 1952 began to look for expansion overseas. In November, armed with around £50,000, he and Fujisawa set off for the USA to buy in the sort of advanced machine tools that he needed for effective mass production.

Back home Honda's expansion continued: a new plant was established at Niikura and the original Tokyo factory became an engine training school for the bicycle dealers who were Honda's principal outlets. Later, in 1953, a labour union was established, and by the end of the year another four-stroke ohv single – the Benly J-Type – was launched using a derivative of the Dream engine. It had a three-speed gearbox, a pressed steel frame and 'see-saw' rear suspension where the engine, drive system and rear wheel pivoted on the frame. It proved to be another instant success.

However, Honda's massive investment and expansion programme nearly led to the downfall of the company. By the end of 1953, the Japanese

Honda's mass market F-type Cub – a 50 cc motorised bicycle of 1952

Above: *the facade of Honda's Kyushu branch in 1953*

Above right: *the Nagoya branch of Honda Motor Company (1954)*

economy was sliding back into recession again as the Korean war ended, and with it America's massive buying sprees in Japan. Running into desperate cash-flow problems and unable to pay for the machine tools he had bought in the USA, Honda turned to his bank for help.

Employees rallied round, working without bonuses or holidays, and an ally in the Mitsubishi Bank, who recognised the enormous potential of Honda's export dreams, was able to keep the company afloat, thus averting a takeover bid.

The year 1954 was a testing time for Honda. Sales of the Cub were falling as the Japanese market demanded something more sophisticated, and buyers were having problems with the newly-introduced two-stroke 200 cc Juno scooter and a 225 cc version of the Dream. The scooter, which used a polyester resin body to enclose the engine, was prone to overheating, while the new Dream proved unreliable. Neither problem was insurmountable and, despite all the crises at home, Honda still pursued his exports goal. The best way to do this, he reasoned, was to make the products famous throughout the world, and what better way to do that than go racing? So in March 1954 he entered a works-prepared Dream in a race in Brazil. It did not do very well, finishing 13th out of 22 starters, but it was a beginning.

The outcome of the race whetted Honda's appetite and he announced that his company would compete in the Isle of Man TT races in 1959, which gave him five years to develop a competitive racer. In June 1954 he set off for the Isle of Man to see the TT races himself, although Honda's visit was principally to check out the European market he hoped to make his own. His first stop was Hamburg, and there he saw scooters and machinery not available in Japan. But he, and Fujisawa who accompanied him, did not see a competitor to the lightweight mass market machine that they hoped to produce.

Honda did not find Britain a particularly welcoming place. He was refused permission to visit a carburettor factory, apparently because memories of the Second World War were still strong. But he did manage to visit one or two works to see how other companies operated. He returned laden with carburettors, spark-plugs, plus all manner of motor cycle paraphernalia. He had also seen the incredible sophistication of the European racers and sought to match their power and speed, establishing a separate design department for this purpose. The announcement of his intention to compete in the TT improved moral at Honda Motor Company, just when it was needed most.

However, Honda still needed the cheap, reliable, practical, clean, economical and attractive machine that he planned to use to spearhead his export bid. For three years he worked on the scheme and then in June 1958 the 50 cc four-stroke Super Cub C100 was announced. It was a revelation. Neither scooter nor motor cycle, the Super Cub was an in-between machine that coined a new word to describe it – scooterette. It was everything Honda had aimed for and it sold in almost unbelievable quantities right from its first production in August 1958. Within 15 years more than 9 million had been sold and proof of the original 'rightness' of the design is the fact that the Super Cub is still alive in the 1980s. Production reached 15 million in April 1983.

Development at Honda was proceeding apace: from 1955 to 1957 Dreams and Benlys were produced in a variety of sizes from 125 to 350 cc. In 1957 Honda's research team developed their first twin-cylinder road bike – an all-aluminium 250 cc machine with a single overhead camshaft and, unusually, both frame, swing arm and front leading link forks were made largely in pressed steel. The bike was the C70 Dream and its lighting, electrics and switch gear were a revelation for most riders. The following year the machine was equipped with an electric starter, and in 1959 the C72 Dream was shown at the Amsterdam show – it would be an understatement to say that the bike was the sensation of the show. This was the beginning of Honda's incredible penetration into Europe. That same year a North American subsidiary was set up in California, and in 1961 another branch in West Germany.

But, of course, Hondas had been exported before 1959. One or two Dreams had been sent to Okinawa back in 1952, when the islands were under American control. And several Juno scooters were exported to the USA as a sort of toe-in-the-water exercise in 1954. The export drive began in earnest in 1957 when Hondas were again exported to Okinawa and throughout South East Asia. In less than 12 months 285 machines were sold abroad.

Honda's first serious exports to the USA were shipped in 1958 – just two units! But the following year, when the Honda subsidiary was established, an initial order of 96 bikes was placed. It was not long before 140 a month were being sold, and in 1962 over 65,000 Hondas were sold in the USA – something like half the total market.

The North American market was the big one for Honda. Dominated for years by large, heavy and high-powered machines such as Harley-Davidsons, there were few lightweight machines available. Honda reasoned that with the post-war boom in the United States many people would turn to motor cycles as a recreational vehicle; he was right! Between 1957 and 1963 North America took almost 35 per cent of Honda's exports; more than 235,000 machines.

Honda's concept of appealing to the sort of people who did not consider themselves motor cyclists but who wanted recreation as well as sensible transport was the key to his big export success. For years British manufacturers had concentrated on enthusiasts, race fans who wanted machines they could tinker with themselves and emulate the racing stars. Of course, Honda wanted to appeal to the traditional type of biker too, but he saw the big sales, the big rewards as coming from a virtually untapped market – so he aimed there first.

A machine of almost unbelievable sophistication for 1961 – the C72 250 cc Dream twin-cylinder tourer

Above: *Soichiro Honda always took a keen interest in all aspects of production. Here he is at the Wako Research and Development plant*

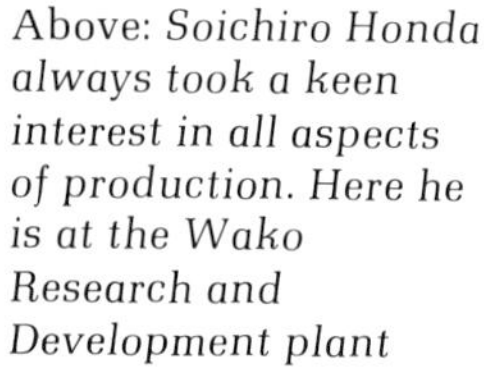

Above, right: *Soichiro Honda astride one of his racing machines at the opening of Honda Benelux near Brussels (1963)*

Opposite, top: *the Super Cub was given an electric starter in 1961 – this is the C102*

Opposite, bottom: *one of the machines that spearheaded Honda's conquest of the British market – the high-performance CB92 Benly 125 cc twin*

The first exports to Europe came to the Netherlands and Britain in 1957, and an importer was established in London shortly afterwards. A few of the early C71s came to Britain, but the big sales were reserved for the C72 which, unlike the C71, had 12-volt electrics and wet-sump lubrication.

The lightweight motor cycle which, together with the C72 and the C100 Super Cub, formed the basis of Honda's first export drive to Europe and the USA was the twin-cylinder ohc C92 Benly, a 125 cc machine. This was launched in April 1959 and first came to the UK in 1960.

Recognising the importance of research and development Honda made the R and D Department completely independent in 1960, and it is now funded with over three per cent of the total Honda income. Honda himself decided that an R and D department would work better as an independent unit, arguing that a manufacturing part demands high production, but R and D must expect 99 per cent of their efforts to end in failure.

In 1961 Honda expanded into the farming market, manufacturing a power tiller. Today the Power Products Division, set up to handle this kind of operation, is one of the fastest growing divisions within Honda.

In 1961, as a flood of new Cubs, Benlys and Dreams were produced, Honda established their first overseas manufacturing plant in Taiwan, off the mainland of China.

In 1963 a subsidiary was established in Belgium to assemble and sell mopeds throughout the Common Market. That same year a 300 cc twin was built – the Dream C78 – and a 90 cc Benly announced. In October Honda's all-conquering C100 Super Cub earned a prestigious French award for engineering excellence – the *Mode Coupe*.

On the motor cycle front Honda fitted an electric starter to one version of the Super Cub – the C102 – in 1961 and later that year marketed a 125 cc version of the original Juno scooter which had failed to catch the public's attention. The new 125, known as the M80, proved to be more successful.

The early Hondas that came to Britain in 1960 were a revelation to riders used to machinery that was prone to leak oil and was often unreliable. The C92 125 cc Benly, for example, had an overhead camshaft engine and proved capable of 70 mph (113 kph) – performance almost equal to several British two-fiftys. And the CB72, the sporty successor to the C72 250 cc twin, was no less outstanding – it was easily capable of 80 mph (128 kph), yet returned a respectable 66 mpg (4.27 litres/100 km) fuel economy.

Improved versions of both machines were announced in Britain in 1961. The sporty CB72 – launched in Japan the previous November – went over to a racey style tubular frame and telescopic front suspension, unlike the earlier model which had had pressed steel forks with a leading link suspension set up.

The fastest and most powerful production Honda to date was the 28.5 bhp 305 cc CB77 Super Sports twin that was launched in Japan in October 1963, some months after the 305 cc tourer, the C77. British road tests showed that the CB77 was more than a match for several bigger British bikes, with 95 mph (152 kph) being readily attainable.

The story of Honda right from the beginning

Right: *to counter the fact that under 50-cc machines are not allowed on British Motorways, Honda introduced, in 1964, this S65 machine with a 65 cc ohc engine*
Opposite, top: *Honda's first 'own-brand' motor – the 50 cc A-type two-stroke clip-on bicycle motor that was unkindly dubbed the 'chimney'*
Opposite, centre: *the four-stroke Benly J-type of 1953 – just 3.8 bhp; not bad from a 90 cc engine of 30 years ago*
Opposite, bottom: *the bike that began a commuter revolution – the Super Cub C100. This one was photographed in 1958*
Below: *this CM90 scooterette is similar to the Super Cub but has a 90 cc engine*

Honda

IN EUROPA 
Dream
MMP 77C
HONDA

has been one of continuous expansion, fuelled by constant development and model changes. There are several reasons for this. One of these was that Fujisawa, the marketing genius who masterminded Honda's expansion overseas, believed that motor cycles were like fashion: they had to keep pace with and/or outstrip people's tastes; any standing still would be fatal. Then, of course, there was Honda's own engineering drive: his constant striving for technical excellence and sophistication. His legacy of constant development is still inextricably bound up in Honda's philosophy. Engineers are still the men who shape Honda's future: at the moment Kiyoshi Kawashima, the engineer-turned-businessman, is the President, and it's likely that his successor will come from the ranks of the engineers too.

Keen to cash in on the big bike market in the USA where, thanks to a sophisticated advertising campaign and a line of attractive products, Honda had already taken over the lightweight market, they launched their biggest bike ever – the CB450 twin. Here was a real engineers' bike – it incorporated novel torsion-bar operated valve springs, double overhead camshafts and an unusual 180 degree throw crankshaft to give better balance.

The bike found instant favour in Britain where it gained almost a cult following, and no wonder for with a speed of 104 mph (166 kph) plus it was faster than many British five-hundreds. But strangely it was something of a failure in the US,

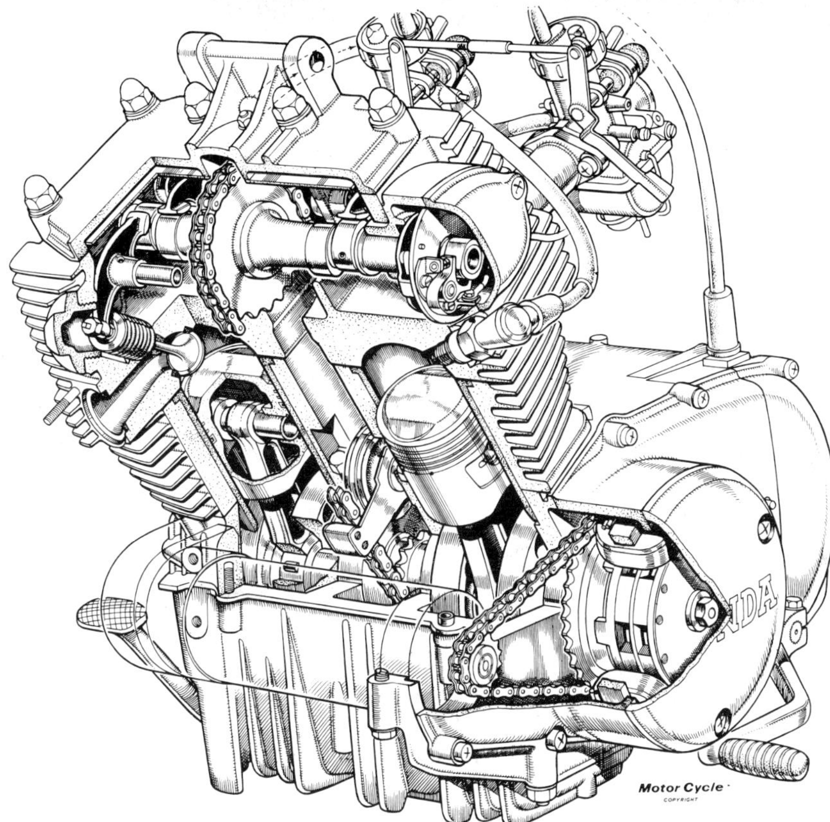

Above: *cut-away view of single overhead cam twin-cylinder CB160 engine. Note the cast lugs on the head – this engine formed a stressed part of the frame*

Opposite, top: *scene stealer at the 1961 Amsterdam Motor Cycle Show was this 305 cc twin-cylinder tourer, the C77*

Below: *at the time it was Honda's biggest roadster – the double overhead cam CB450 twin. This sporty machine proved more than a match for many British five-hundreds but failed to sell in the numbers envisaged*

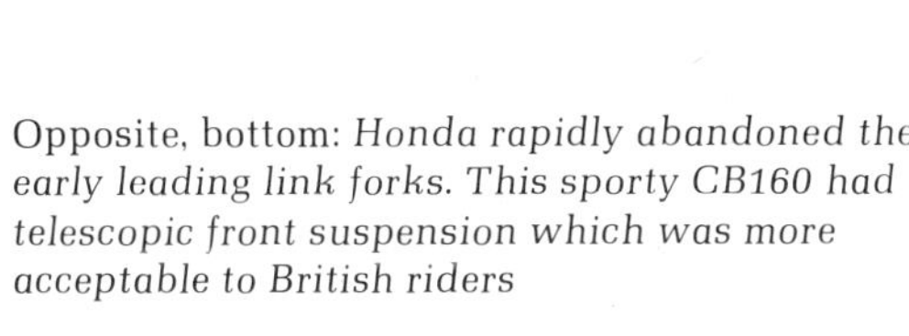

Opposite, bottom: *Honda rapidly abandoned the early leading link forks. This sporty CB160 had telescopic front suspension which was more acceptable to British riders*

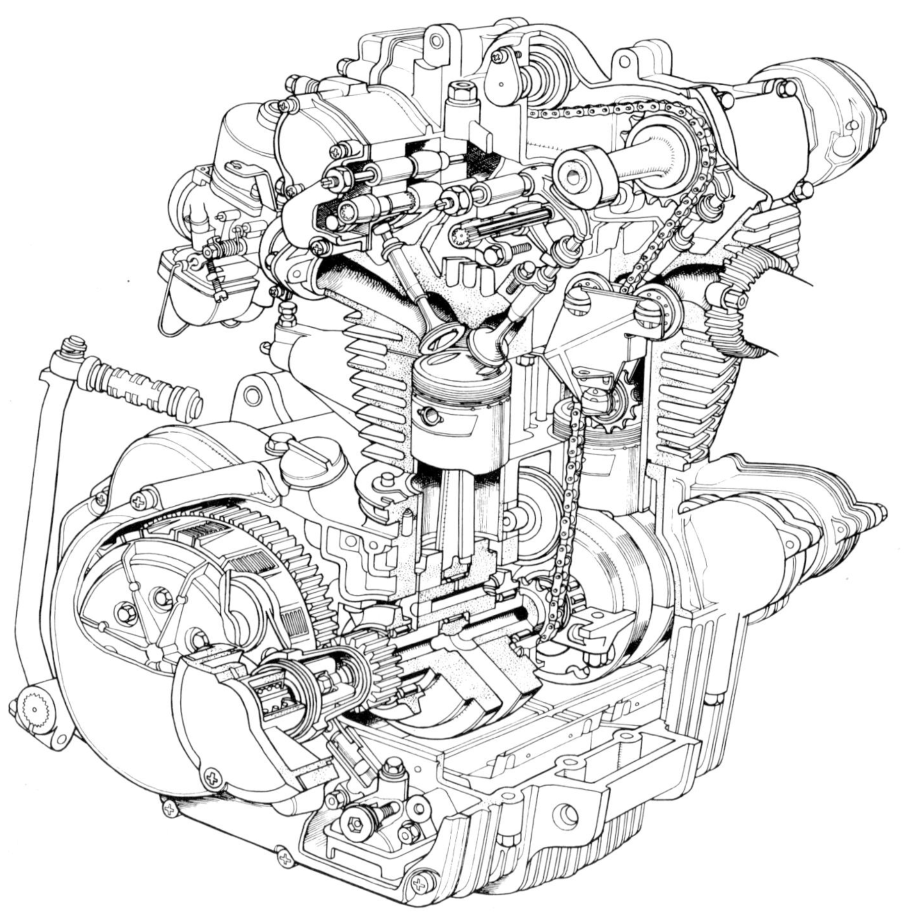

Power unit of the CB450 was innovative. Note the 'one up one down' crank and torsion bar valve springs

Opposite: *the 10 millionth Honda – a CB450 ridden off the assembly line by Soichiro Honda in 1968*

the very market it was aimed at. Its four-speed-only gearbox incorporated awkward ratios and, despite the new crank, it did vibrate. It was redesigned in 1967 with different carburettors and a five-speed gearbox, and though much improved, it had perhaps come a little late to recoup lost sales. The model was finally withdrawn in 1970.

With Honda's withdrawal from the road-racing grands prix in 1967, the R and D Department was able to devote its entire efforts towards production machinery which now included portable generators, cars, pick-up trucks and a whole host of agricultural equipment.

For 1968 Honda's technicians came up with a completely new set of 250 cc and 350 cc twins – the CB250 and CB350, both of which had five-speed gearboxes. These machines replaced the old CB72 and CB77 bikes.

In January of 1968 Honda's total motor cycle production had reached the astonishing total of 10 million units. That 10 millionth machine, a CB450, was ridden off the assembly line by Soichiro himself. The record book shows that of those 10 million machines 2,750,000 had been exported to more than 135 countries – a fine achievement for a company that had been in existence less than 20 years.

Honda's marketing foresight which showed that big bike sales would rocket as the 1960s came to a close, coupled with the development department's keenness to produce a four-cylinder roadster using some of the engineering expertise gained with the racing fours, spawned a 'superbike' project. This project was probably begun in earnest early in 1967, but, despite hints and rumours when the machine was launched in October 1968 at the Tokyo Show, the motor cycling world was stunned. The machine was so big, so powerful and so sophisticated that a new word had to be coined to describe it – superbike.

The bike, was, of course, the CB750 four – an overhead camshaft machine with electric starting and a power output of nearly 70 bhp. When this 737 cc machine was tested for the first time by the British weekly paper *Motor Cycle* it proved to be the quickest machine going. Its top speed was close on 120 mph (190 kph), but the acceleration was the most impressive feature – over the quarter-mile the CB750 recorded a time of 12.6 seconds and 102 mph (163 kph). Nothing else could live with that.

The bike began the whole superbike craze of the late 1960s and 1970s that is only now showing signs of petering out. The CB750 was more powerful than the Triumph Trident – then the most advanced British superbike.

Over the ten years that the CB750 was in production engineering and styling changes were few and far between – it was obviously right first time. Total sales were no less than 1 million over the same period.

Honda's own ideas of management have been revolutionary and not at all like those of the traditional Japanese. He was often to be seen on the shop floor working away with his staff, but he managed to combine respect with fear. At times his rages went out of control and he has been known to hit his employees; on several occasions when an employee has made a mistake Honda hit them over the head with whatever tools were to hand! However, unlike most Japanese company bosses he never expected automatic and unquestioning loyalty and respect. 'If somebody says he works out of loyalty to the company he is a damned liar. Everybody must work for himself. Even I work because I like working,' he once said.

Even so Honda was hurt and confused by the workers strike of 1957 at the Shirako and Yamato plants. The workers were campaigning for a bigger wage rise, partly because much of the Japanese industry was in recession and partly because the company had given generous settlements after the voluntary wage restraint during the 1954 crisis. The dispute was eventually settled but it had a sobering effect on Honda, and although he personally stayed aloof from the whole business it's worth mentioning, as an illustration of his approach, that when he discovered that some management personnel had started printing posters saying 'the Company has won' he went mad and ordered them destroyed. 'You fools,' he told them. 'This is no battlefield.'

The CB750 started a whole flood of four-cylinder Hondas beginning with the CB350F in 1972 (never imported into Britain) and continuing into the 1980s though the emphasis is now on

1000万台突破
ホンダ二輪車
本田技研浜松製作所

Editor Mick Woollett tries out the world's first real superbike– the CB750 of 1969

vee-engine configurations as opposed to in-line layouts.

In 1969 Honda opened up subsidiaries in Australia and Canada, and by August of that year total bike production had reached the staggering figure of 12,237,497.

The next year Honda began production of a novel type of three-wheeler recreational vehicle – they called it ATC (All Terrain Cycle). The first bike – the ATC90 – was only exported to the USA, and today there are many variants of these balloon-tyred machines – in some states of the USA they are selling faster than two-wheelers.

Again in 1970 Honda launched their first 125 cc four-stroke single for years – the CB125S – and the same year announced new production and export records: 14 million machines produced since 1948; in November they produced 165,489 machines, setting a new monthly record.

In 1971 Kawashima was appointed President of Honda R and D Ltd – now a completely separate company and the new CB500 four was announced. By the middle of 1972 Honda UK had captured 50 per cent of the total British bike market . . . in just ten years.

It was Fujisawa who brought about Honda's retirement in 1973, though the company's founder had been working his way around to retirement, precipitated perhaps by several things that brought home to him the need to hand over the reins to someone younger. After all, he had pioneered the Honda philosophy that youth should be entrusted with responsibility to keep the ideas fresh.

Fujisawa had become tired, despite his age of just 62 – Honda was four years older – so when Fujisawa told the board of directors that he wished to retire, Honda announced that both men should retire on the twenty-fifth anniversary of the company's founding . . . in September 1973.

Though both officially retired, each was given the title of Director and Supreme Advisor, though neither had any responsibility to make managerial decisions.

Honda was philosophical about his retirement: 'Not all of the dreams I had at the founding of the company have come true,' he said. 'Mistakes have been made and my successors will say to me: "Even you have made mistakes". After all I am human!'

In the year that Honda and Fujisawa retired, the RSC (Racing Services Centre) was established to look after the semi-works Honda racing teams all over the world who carried on in competition despite Honda's official withdrawal from the sport. Kawashima became President in October and as part of the company's commitment to engineering development a second new R and D centre was established at Asaka. The following year Honda's engineers were dispatched abroad for the first time to complete their training by gaining a broader view of the world markets.

A new dimension in long-distance touring motor cycles was created in 1974 when the water-cooled GL1000 Gold Wing was marketed in October. It was the first Honda to have water-cooling, perhaps because Soichiro Honda himself had always believed (until shortly before his retirement) that air-cooled engines are technically superior. The 'Wing with its flat-four engine and shaft-drive set new standards in smoothness, comfort and quiet -running. When it was launched it really was the ultimate, though perhaps with recent development into water-cooled engines and even turbocharged machinery it now seems a little dated.

A new factory at Kumamoto was opened in January 1976 and the highly successful Express two-stroke moped launched the next month. Motor cycle production was begun in Brazil that year and the first big bike with an efficient automatic torque converter transmission – the CB750 Hondamatic – went on sale. In July a big new test track was established at Tochigi to complement the Suzuka circuit built in 1962 for international road race events.

In 1977, mindful of the possibility of future import controls, a big new 217-acre production plant was established in Ohio, USA to build machines like the Gold Wing.

That same year two extraordinary Hondas made their appearance: the water-cooled CX500 V-twin and the fabulous CBX1000 six. The two machines were poles apart: the CX500 was a machine designed to be quiet, efficient,

Honda were first with three-wheel off-road fun bikes and coined the name ATC for All Terrain Cycle. This 250 cc model is being tried out by Ron Haslam

maintenance-free (well, almost) and pollution-free. In effect it was a foretaste of the sort of motor cycles everyone would be riding as the pollution and noise controls became ever stricter towards the end of the 20th century.

The CBX on the other hand was a six-cylinder 105 bhp machine with twin overhead camshafts and four valves per cylinder. More than anything else, this was a bike with a grand prix racing pedigree. At 130 mph (208 kph) plus, it was the fastest bike around, but sadly it did not seem to fit in with Honda's overall design philosophy and never sold really well. Unfortunately handling was not of a very high standard either and very little development work was done on the bike until 1981 when it was given a new suspension set-up. Production ceased in 1982.

Bike development proceeded faster than ever with the two R and D facilities working flat out: a turbocharged CX500 was launched in 1981, and if anything was a monument to Honda's technological pre-eminence this was it. The bike had everything, including an on-board computer to control the fuel injection and ignition. It also had a self-diagnostic capacity. If one part of the system failed, another could take over.

The machines of the 1980s run from 50 cc mini-bikes and three-cylinder, water-cooled two strokes, through water-cooled V-twins and fours, to air-cooled fours with hydraulic devices to take up tappet clearances (a world first for motor cycles). It is a dazzling array of technological sophistication – Soichiro Honda must be pleased.

The Early Racing Years

The start of one of Mike Hailwood's greatest races as he pushes the 500 cc Honda into life at the 1967 Senior TT. He won the race and shattered the lap record

As early as 1954 Soichiro Honda committed the factory to racing in Europe – despite the fact that at that time Honda exported no machines further than a few hundred miles from Japan and the name Honda was unknown outside Asia.

That of course was the point. What better way of establishing the name and proving the product than by success in racing? In any case the down to earth boss of Honda loved the technical challenge of racing and had himself built and raced a succession of cars in the 1930s.

The first, which some 50 years later went on display at the Honda International Technical School, was powered by a surplus American airforce 8-litre, V8 unit slotted into a chassis which Soichiro (then working in the car trade) built.

The last, built for the 1936 season, was far more sophisticated. Realising that races are won by a combination of power and handling he fitted the Ford V8 engine with a supercharger and tilted it to the left to improve weight distribution for the speedway-style left-handed ovals then popular in Japan for car racing.

The end of his own racing career came in July 1936. Leading an important race on a circuit near Tokyo he came upon a hazard known to all who have raced – the slow tail-enders about to be lapped. Carved-up in no uncertain fashion Honda's car rolled three times and flung him out.

His injuries, including serious facial abrasions and a broken left shoulder and wrist, took almost two years to heal completely. His only consolation was that the lap record he set that day on the Tama River course remained unbroken for ten years.

So racing was in Soichiro's blood. And in addition to spreading the name Honda and proving the product he realised something European manufacturers tended to ignore – that a successful racing programme was the best way to boost the morale of the factory workers.

Speaking of his decision to go racing he said: 'Most of the workers at that time were so young that they were attracted to the idea of winning races . . . particularly because we had just lost the war, the idea of hoisting the Japanese flag on the Isle of Man gave them real excitement. It really stirred their blood.'

It was not that Honda had money to spare. In fact the infant factory, struggling for survival amid a mass of motor cycle manufacturers who had mushroomed into being during the post-war boom, was rocked by one financial crisis after another in the early 1950s as the boom faded.

Leaving the money problems to his partner Takeo Fujisawa, Honda flew to the Isle of Man to spectate at the 1954 TT races. Two shocks were in store for him. First the strong anti-Japanese feeling of the British people, many of whom had suffered at the hands of the Japanese during the war which had finished less than nine years before his visit. Second the strength of the opposition that Honda would have to face when they entered the world arena of motor cycle racing.

That year Ray Amm on a works Norton won the Senior from Geoff Duke (Gilera) but old timers will remember that the race was cut short because of appalling weather conditions. Rod Coleman of New Zealand took the 350 cc honours for AJS but what obviously impressed the Japanese visitor most were the works NSUs that swept the board in both the 125 cc and 250 cc races.

For the design of the beautifully engineered West German engines with their short-stroke, high revving layout coincided closely with his own ideas of the way to extract maximum power from a given capacity.

However, their power output (17 bhp for the single-cylinder 125 cc NSU on which Rupert Hollaus won the Ultra Lightweight TT and 33 bhp for the twin ridden to victory by Werner Haas in the 250 cc race) made him wonder if he had been wise to tell his workers that Honda would race in Europe – for it was some three-times the power of the early Honda sports models.

He was also impressed by various European components that were clearly superior to the Japanese equivalents of 1954 – in particular chains, tyres and carburettors. So impressed that he decided to take samples home with him, arriving at Rome airport for the return flight way over the weight limit.

A hot tempered man he had a furious row when the check-in staff refused to allow him to board unless he paid for his excess baggage. It could not

ASTROL
Cast
4
HONDA
4

The Honda team pose outside the Nursery Hotel in Onchan during their first visit to the TT in 1959. Kneeling in front is Kiyoshi Kawashima, now President of the company

be resolved by him simply paying because he had run out of money – and in any case it seemed illogical to him that he, a small wiry man, should pay the same as a fatter person weighing twice as much. Eventually the deadlock was resolved by him unpacking his suitcase and putting on several layers of clothes thus lightening his luggage.

It took Honda five years to fulfil the dream of competing in the Isle of Man TT races – and truth to tell it was not the epoch making debut that those not old enough to remember it might imagine, for you have to realise that Honda were the pioneers. Up to their appearance in Europe Japanese goods had always been thought of as second-best, often cheap copies of European or American designs that were shoddily made and of poor quality. The flood of high quality cameras, televisions, hi-fi equipment, cars and motor cycles was yet to come.

The first definite mention of Honda's participation in the 1959 TT to be made in Europe was in *The Motor Cycle* (now *Motor Cycle Weekly*) dated 5 February 1959, which reported that Ichiro Niitsuma of the technical department and William Hunt, an American adviser and racer, had called at the London office of the British Auto-Cycle Union to discuss Honda's participation in the TT.

There was some confusion at first because at that time there were Formula Races in the TT for production racing machines (as opposed to works specials) and Honda wanted to field their 125 cc bikes in this class. However, only two Formula races were in the programme – for 350 cc and 500 cc machines. This forced Honda to enter the open 125 cc Ultra Lightweight TT where they faced the established might of the Italian MV Agusta and Ducati teams as well as the fast-rising East German MZ squad.

Honda were further handicapped by fielding riders with no Isle of Man experience (four Japanese plus their American adviser Hunt) although Honda himself knew that to win they would have to employ established star riders. Speaking to an interviewer he said: 'The rider is equally important as the machine. If we had a machine with the same level of performance as those of our competitors, we wouldn't win the race without a top-notch rider.'

In fact the 1959 Honda 125 cc racers were not as powerful as the MV Agusta, Ducati and MZ opposition. But they were beautifully engineered and very reliable and by finishing sixth, seventh and eighth carried off the team prize.

However, this success, which boosted morale at the factory, did not blind Mr Honda to the fact that his leading rider, Naomi Taniguchi, had averaged only 68.29 mph (109.90 kph) for the ten laps of the short Clypse circuit compared to Tarquinio Provini's winning average of 74.06 mph (119.9 kph) on a factory single-cylinder MV Agusta. In fact Taniguchi had finished over 7 minutes behind the winner. A lot had been achieved – but an awful lot remained to be done before Honda could compete and win.

Above: *Honda's most successful rider on their first visit to the Isle of Man TT in 1959 was Naomi Taniguchi here seen at the Nursery Bends on the Clypse course on his way to sixth place in the 125 cc event*

Left: *another picture from 1959, Honda's first year at the Isle of Man TT. Here Tanaka returns to the Honda base-camp at the Nursery Hotel after unofficial practice. Kiyoshi Kawashima looks on*

HONDA
1

2
HONDA
2

The 1959 Honda 125 cc racers were powered by twin-cylinder (44 × 41 mm bore and stroke) engines that revved to 13,000 rpm and produced 18 hp. With shaft-driven, double overhead camshafts they had a distinct NSU look about them although there was no question of the Honda being a copy – the layout was different, and in any case the West German factory, who quit racing at the end of 1954, had never raced a twin in the 125 cc class.

The gearbox was a six-speeder and the Keihin racing carburettors proved that the Japanese could do more than just copy for they had flat slides compared to the cylindrical slides used by all the European machines. Other features included a welded spine frame and a leading link front fork.

At that time the Isle of Man TT was far and away the most important motor cycle race of the year. After competing the Honda team went straight home – and work on the 1960 effort started.

Rumours of a four-cylinder 250 cc Honda spread and were confirmed when the factory fielded a team of five in a race in Japan in August 1959. They swept the board and Honda set about preparing a full-scale invasion of Europe with teams of both 125 cc and 250 cc machines to contest not only the TT but several of the European Grands Prix as well.

The team appeared for the first time in 1960 at the TT with redesigned 125 cc twins and the brand new 250 cc four-cylinder machines. These were powered by double overhead camshaft, in-line across-the-frame engines with the same bore and stroke as the 125 cc (44 × 41 mm) and produced about 35 bhp at 14,000 rpm.

Again the results were far from impressive. Both races were back on the full 37.7-mile (60.7-km) Mountain circuit, and in addition to their Japanese riders Honda enlisted the help of Australians Bob Brown and Tom Phillis.

In the smaller class Taniguchi was again their best rider – and again he was sixth, way behind the winning MV Agustas of Carlo Ubbiali and Gary Hocking. The 250 cc was more impressive. It was obviously fast but the handling simply was not good enough though Bob Brown battled on to finish fourth with other Hondas ridden by Kitano and Taniguchi fifth and sixth, a long long way behind the MV Agusta twins of winner Hocking and runner-up Ubbiali.

For the Dutch TT Honda signed a man who was to become synonymous with Honda successes – London born Jim Redman, who spent his schooldays in Rhodesia and later settled in South Africa. He finished fourth in the 125 cc race and seventh in the 250 cc – first Honda home in both. The Belgian Grand Prix a week later proved a disaster and the German event was even worse for Bob Brown was killed while riding the 250 cc machine during practising.

Despite this setback Tanaka took third place in the 250 cc race – Honda's best performance to date. Redman followed up with a third in the 250 cc class at the Ulster Grand Prix and then proved beyond doubt the potential of the machine by taking second place in the final grand prix of the year at Monza in Italy in September at an average speed of 107.37 mph (172.79 kph) –

Opposite, top: *action from the 1964 Ulster Grand Prix as Jim Redman heads for victory in the 350 cc race*

Opposite, bottom: *one of Ralph Bryans' last races for Honda was at Oulton Park in September 1968. Here he is seen in action on a five-cylinder 125 cc Honda*

Australian Tom Phillis was one of the first to really put Honda on the racing map. Here he heads for second place in the 250 cc Ulster Grand Prix of 1960

In 1961 the famous Scot Bob McIntyre raced works Hondas. Here he sits astride a 250 cc machine; Honda captain Jim Redman is standing next to him (centre)

Opposite: *Mike Hailwood is seen here competing on a factory four-cylinder 250 cc Honda in the French Grand Prix of 1961. It was his first ever world championship outing for Honda and he finished second to team-mate Tom Phillis*

beaten only by World Champion Carlo Ubbiali (MV Agusta).

During their two year 'apprenticeship' Honda had learned a great deal and, despite their 10,000-mile (16,000-km) line of communication, proved they could compete in the top class – although they still had to win.

As the Honda star was rising with buoyant sales at home and in South East Asia so the European industry was in the grip of recession. Both MV Agusta and Ducati dropped out and so the sporting world was denied the chance of seeing Honda taking on the top European firms in a battle of giants in 1962.

In fact MV Agusta had decided to concentrate their efforts in the 350 cc and 500 cc classes where the competition was weaker and where they were confident that their well established four-cylinder racers could still win without spending a fortune on development. Their rider Gary Hocking had a single outing on a works 250 cc MV Agusta – at the season-opening Spanish Grand Prix at Barcelona.

The twisty short circuit around Montjuich Park was ideal for Hocking and the MV Agusta twin. He won the race from Tom Phillis (Honda), Silvio Grasetti (Benelli) and Jim Redman (Honda), while at the same meeting Phillis took the 125 cc race to record Honda's first ever win in a World Championship Grand Prix event.

Phillis went on to win the 1961 125 cc title after a tremendous battle with Ernst Degner (MZ) that went to the final round of the contest in Argentina. But the Australian was not the first to clinch a road racing World Championship for Honda. That honour went to the man many consider to be the greatest racing motor cyclist of all time: Mike Hailwood.

Although not an official factory rider Hailwood, who celebrated his 21st birthday in April that year, was lent works machines early in the year: first a 250 cc for the French Grand Prix at Clermont-Ferrand, where he finished second to Phillis, then a 125 cc and a 250 cc for the Isle of Man TT – the race that Soichiro Honda wanted to win above all others. 'Only by winning at the Isle of Man can we open our way toward becoming a world enterprise and to selling our products internationally.'

Imagine his delight when Hailwood won both races at record speed! Honda in fact took the first five places in both events. The Japanese factory had truly arrived – and Hailwood and the Honda team went on to dominate the 250 cc class; Honda machines winning ten of the 11 250 cc World Championship rounds held that year!

Not content to rest on their laurels Honda expanded their racing effort for 1962. They moved downward into the new 50 cc classes and up into the 350 cc division to contest four of the five solo World Championships. But one man absent from their line-up was Hailwood. He had been offered a contract by Count Domenico Agusta to race the factory MV Agusta machines in the 350 cc and 500 cc classes and had accepted.

The official works riders that year were Jim Redman, who was in effect the captain of the team, Tom Phillis, Scot Bob McIntyre, Swiss Luigi Taveri, who had joined Honda from MV Agusta the previous year, Ireland's Tommy Robb and the talented Japanese Kunimitsu Takahashi with Tanaka coming over for the last few races.

Additionally Honda continued their policy of lending works machines to some of their importers who were free to lend them to top riders – a good move because it generated a lot of local publicity. However, it also caused a lot of ill feeling in the Isle of Man when Derek Minter, riding for the British Honda importer of the time, went out and won the race, beating Honda captain Jim Redman against team orders.

Taveri won the 125 cc for Honda but the factory's move up into the 350 cc race with a four-cylinder machine bored out to 285 cc started with a tragedy. Quiet-spoken Australian Tom Phillis was killed when he crashed in the Laurel Bank section while chasing Hailwood and Hocking on the two works MV Agustas.

Despite being badly shaken by the death of his closest friend Redman won the next four 350 cc races in succession, beating Hailwood and the MV Agusta, to win the World Championship at

41
HONDA

Honda's first attempt. He also won six 250 cc Grands Prix to take the quarter-litre crown. Rounding off their most successful year so far the Honda team won ten of the 11 125 cc rounds to make it three titles in the bag with Taveri the 125 cc champion. Only in the 50 cc class were they beaten, with Ernst Degner (Suzuki) and Hans-Georg Anscheidt (Kreidler) finishing ahead of Taveri.

In 1963 the opposition began to stiffen. The Suzuki factory, who had followed Honda's pioneering move into European racing, fielded strong teams of two-strokes in the 50 cc and 125 cc classes while Yamaha became definite challengers in the 250 cc category with their very fast RD56 two-stroke twin. The Italian Morini factory also challenged strongly, fielding former MV Agusta and Mondial star Tarquinio Provini on a very light and fast single-cylinder four-stroke.

Soichiro Honda revelled in the challenge. He realised that strong opposition would not only stimulate his designers, development engineers and riders but that it would also result in better publicity. For, as he used to tell team captain Jim Redman: 'You must have indians as well as cowboys.' In other words it was far better to compete against strong opposition even if it meant losing occasionally rather than score hollow victories.

The massive team of the previous year was trimmed to a more manageable size. Redman was supported by Taveri and Robb and the team concentrated on the 125, 250 and 350 cc classes. Hugh Anderson and the disc valve two-stroke Suzuki proved too fast to catch in the 125 cc races but Redman fought and won two long-running battles to keep his 250 cc and 350 cc crowns.

In the smaller class it was a desperately close run thing with Redman eventually beating Provini on the lone Morini by just two points. In the 350 cc class he beat Hailwood and MV Agusta by four points. It had been a tough year and it was obvious that Honda would need radical new machines if they were to stem the rising tide of two-strokes.

Pouring millions of yen into their 1964 race-development programme Honda built three completely new machines for the 50 cc, 125 cc and 250 cc classes – and produced an extensively revamped model for the 350 cc category.

The single-cylinder 50 cc engine was replaced by a double overhead camshaft twin with bore and stroke of 33 × 29.2 mm that peaked at an astronomical 20,000 rpm – far higher than any racing engine had ever revved before. The 125 cc twin was superseded by an across-the-frame four, a scaled down version of the successful 250 cc engine with bore and stroke of 35 × 32 mm that developed 25 bhp at 16,000 rpm.

The 50 cc machine still was not fast enough (despite their ten-speed gearboxes) to combat the

Above: *Mike Hailwood on his way to victory in the 1961 125 cc Isle of Man TT. He was the first man to win a TT for Honda*

Opposite, top: *classic style from Mike Hailwood as he cranks a 250 cc six-cylinder Honda to yet another win at Mallory Park in 1968*

Opposite, bottom: *a masterpiece of miniaturisation, the eight-speed, 16,000 rpm 250 cc six measured no more across the fairing than did the singles of its day. No grand-prix bike ever had a more haunting exhaust note*

Following pages: *the two men who put Honda on the racing map – Jim Redman (leading) and Tom Phillis at Mallory Park in 1961. Redman is on a 1961 250 cc four while Phillis rides a 1960 machine*

HONDA
2

HONDA
1

two-stroke Suzukis but Taveri regained his 125 cc world title on the new four. The 250 cc turned out to be the toughest class of the year with Redman, who started the season on a four-cylinder model, battling with Phil Read who had joined Yamaha at the end of 1963 to race their simple but incredibly fast RD56 two-stroke twin.

Early in the year Redman did well and opened up a lead in the championship by winning the Isle of Man and Dutch TTs. Then Read hit back with three consecutive successes in East Germany, West Germany and Ulster. By finishing second in all three Redman kept the Honda challenge alive – but he had to win the class at the Italian Grand Prix over the ultra-fast Monza circuit if he was to retain the title.

By that time the four-cylinder model was no match for the Yamaha on the fast circuits, so given the choice of the four or the as yet un-raced and top secret six-cylinder machine, Redman decided to gamble on the new bike. It proved a sensation when it was wheeled out for practising, the across-the-frame air-cooled, double overhead camshaft engine amazingly compact and possessing a truly musical exhaust note as the revs wailed up through the gears to the 17,000 rpm maximum – and beyond when hard pressed.

It looked as though the gamble would pay off when Redman led the race in the early stages but then the engine began to overheat, lost power and slowed, letting the jubilant Read through to win the race and the 250 cc title. Redman had some

Above: *Australian Tom Phillis (Honda) chases Ernst Degner (MZ) in the 125 cc class of the 1961 Austrian Grand Prix*

Right: *during 1964 Jim Redman (Honda) fought a series of battles with Yamaha's Phil Read. Here Redman leads his rival during the German Grand Prix at Solitude*

Above: dramatic shot of Tom Phillis as the suspension of his Honda bottoms-out as he hits the bottom of Bray Hill during the 1962 250 cc TT. He finished third

Left: Honda's lightweight stars in action in the 1964 125 cc Ulster Grand Prix with Luigi Taveri leading from Ralph Bryans

Above: *the crowd at Parliament Square, Ramsey get a close up as Jim Redman heads for victory in the 250 cc TT of 1965*

Opposite, top: *mighty machine. Honda stepped up into the 500 cc class for the first time in 1966. Here Jim Redman waits while the Honda mechanics prepare the machine for its debut in the German Grand Prize at Hockenheim*

Opposite, bottom: *Mike Hailwood in action on the famous 250 cc six-cylinder Honda at the 1967 French Grand Prix at Clermont-Ferrand. He lost this race – but won the world championship*

consolation in the 350 cc class in which he won all eight World Championship rounds.

In 1965 the battle between the Honda four-strokes and the Yamaha and Suzuki two-strokes continued in the smaller classes and a European dimension was added when the Italian MV Agusta factory rejoined the 350 cc fray with an interesting new bike powered by a three-cylinder, four-stroke engine.

Ireland's Ralph Bryans put Honda on top in the smallest class but the 125 cc four-cylinder model which had proved so successful the previous year was completely out-classed by Suzuki's new water-cooled, two-stroke twins which finished first and second in the table ridden by Hugh Anderson and Frank Perris.

Honda also took a hammering in the 250 cc class in which Read and Canadian Mike Duff on improved versions of the RD56 twin took first and second places ahead of Redman. But the gritty Rhodesian battled away to win the 350 cc crown for the fourth year in succession despite the tremendous challenge of Hailwood and his young team-mate Giacomo Agostini on the works MV Agustas.

In fact the MV Agusta riders went to Japan for the final round with Agostini leading the championship. And he looked set to take the title when he quickly established what looked to be a winning lead – only to be robbed of victory by a broken contact breaker spring! Hailwood won the 350 cc race for the Italian factory – and the 250 cc event on a factory six-cylinder Honda. That set the tongues wagging and sure enough, Hailwood, who had won his first world title on a Honda back in 1961, joined the Honda team for the 1966 season.

The scene was set for Honda's greatest ever grand prix challenge. For they decided to contest all the solo classes – moving up into the 500 cc division as well as continuing their efforts in the 50 cc, 125 cc, 250 cc and 350 cc. It was the first and only time that one manufacturer has attempted to win all five solo classes.

Honda retained Luigi Taveri and Ralph Bryans to race the 50 cc and 125 cc machines – the smaller bike an improved version of the successful twin, and the 125 cc powered by an incredible five-cylinder engine. Bore and stroke were 33 × 20.2 mm and the 1966 version revved to an ear-splitting 20,000 rpm and produced close to 35 bhp.

Riders for the three bigger classes were Hailwood and Redman with Stuart Graham and Rhodesian Bruce Beale in reserve and getting the occasional ride. Their mounts were an up-rated six-cylinder for the 250 cc class and a new six-cylinder machine for the 350 cc grands prix in which the MV Agusta had proved such a threat the previous year.

This bigger six was in fact an enlarged 250 cc engine with a bore and stroke of 41 × 37.5 mm to give an exact capacity of 296 cc. Power was an impressive 65 bhp at 17,000 rpm. And for their debut in the 500 cc class Honda decided to follow convention and race a four-cylinder machine. It was a multi-million pound effort that came within an ace of total success.

In fact Honda did win all five Manufacturers World Championships – but only three of the more important (from the publicity point of view) individual riders' titles.

Hailwood succeeded brilliantly in the 250 cc class winning all ten grands prix and decisively defeating defending title holder Phil Read (Yamaha). And Hailwood won the 350 cc crown too, winning six races – double the number of successes scored by runner-up Giacomo Agostini (MV Agusta).

But the Italian gained sweet revenge in the more important 500 cc class. There the Honda effort faltered – largely because Redman, who had decided to retire at the end of the year, wanted to go out in a blaze of glory by taking the 500 cc title.

As he was number one for the class Redman rode the only machine that Honda managed to get ready for the opening classic – the West German Grand Prix at the ultra-fast Hockenheim circuit. He made a promising start by winning the race after a great battle with Agostini.

HONDA
HONDA
ONGLIFE BP 
M.HAILWOOD
HONDA

Plug changing time during practising for the 1967 Belgian Grand Prix. Machines are 250 cc six-cylinder models and the rider is Ireland's Ralph Bryans

Redman went further ahead by beating Agostini at the Dutch TT but then came disaster in Belgium when Redman came off during a rain-sodden race. He injured his shoulder – and never raced for Honda again. Three grands prix out of the nine holding the 500 cc class had been run; Agostini led the world championship and Hailwood, left as Honda's sole challenger, had not scored a single point.

Despite his involvement with the 250 cc and 350 cc classes Hailwood did his best, beating Agostini in Czechoslovakia, Ulster and the Isle of Man (the race was run late that year because a seaman's strike had forced the organisers to abandon the traditional June date) and going to Monza for the Italian Grand Prix, final round of the 1966 World Championships, virtually level pegging. There he was bitterly disappointed when gearbox trouble put him out, leaving Agostini to win race and title.

Taveri regained his 125 cc crown to make it three individual titles for Honda but team-mate Bryans lost the 50 cc championship to German Hans-Georg Anscheidt (Suzuki). However, Honda had won all five Manufacturers World Championships – a stupendous achievement. But was it really necessary to field such a massive effort? The world now knew about Honda – and what they could do. With motor cycle sales dropping it was no surprise when the factory decided to drastically cut their race programme for 1967.

They pulled out of the 50 cc and 125 cc classes completely but agreed to support Hailwood and Ralph Bryans in the 250 cc and 350 cc races and to give Hailwood another chance to take the 500 cc crown. So from the massed attack of earlier years the Honda challenge had been slimmed down to just two riders – and team leader Hailwood was involved in two epic season-long struggles that both ended with the Honda rider tieing on points with his rivals!

Hailwood easily took the 350 cc title, winning six of the eight Grands Prix, but it was a very different matter in the 250 cc and 500 cc classes. In the smaller engine division he fought yet another pitched battle with Phil Read – Mike on the latest six-cylinder four-stroke Honda and Phil mounted on a lighter and lower version of the water-cooled, four-cylinder, two-stroke Yamaha.

That year the 250 cc class was decided over 13 rounds and both finished with 50 points, Hailwood taking the title because he had five wins to Read's four. The 500 cc class was even closer – both Hailwood and Agostini (on the three-cylinder MV Agusta) scored 46 points during the ten race series (the points system in those days was very different from today's with just 8 points for a win, 6 for second place, then 4, 3, 2 and 1 for the next four riders to finish). Also, they both had the same number of wins – five apiece. So the number of second places had to be taken into account – and Agostini with three to Hailwood's two came out on top and kept the title he had won the previous year.

Battle of the giants in 1967 as Giacomo Agostini (MV Agusta) leads Mike Hailwood (Honda) during the 500 cc class of the Dutch TT. Hailwood won the race

One consolation for Hailwood and Honda was their win in the Senior TT, reckoned by many to be the most exciting race in the long history of the Isle of Man classic. For 170 miles there was only a few seconds in it. Then, on the fifth lap when the timekeepers had them virtually level pegging, the chain of Agostini's MV Agusta jumped the sprockets leaving Hailwood to win unchallenged and with a record lap at 107.75 mph (173.40 kph) that stood for ten years! Earlier in the week Hailwood had won both the 250 cc and 350 cc TT.

In fact it is worth pausing to ponder over the skill and stamina of Mike the Bike. For example, at the 1967 Dutch TT he rode in three classes (250, 350 and 500 cc) and won them all! How many of todays aces would like to try and emulate that ..

However, out in the great wide world away from racing, things were not going so well. Sales in North America had dropped dramatically causing one of several financial hiccups that punctuated Honda's early years and it was decided to pull out of World Championship racing so that all available resources could be concentrated on the design and development of new roadsters aimed at stimulating and regaining those lost markets.

So Honda's first era of grand prix racing came to a close. Statistics can be dull but it is worth recording that during the seven years of their main effort (1961 to 1967 inclusive) they won 18 manufacturers World Championship titles and their riders took 17 individual World Championship titles. To do this Honda machines won a grand total of 140 grands prix during those years despite fierce opposition from factory machines fielded by Yamaha, Suzuki, MV Agusta, MZ, Morini, Benelli, Bultaco, Kreidler, Aermacchi, Ossa, Derbi, Jawa, Bianchi, EMC, Bridgestone, Vostok, Montesa, CZ, Gilera, AJS, Matchless and Mondial. And that is an average of 20 grand prix wins a year ...

The Grand Prix Machines

When Honda planted their first exploratory foot on the bottom rung of the world-championship ladder in 1959, even they – for all their ambition and determination – could have had no inkling of the spectacular impact they were soon to make. Even the statistics, impressive as they are, cannot evoke the full flavour and tingling excitement that characterised the classic road-racing scene throughout the following years – during which Honda, in the face of fierce competition, collected 18 manufacturers' championships, 16 individual titles and 137 grand-prix victories, including 18 Isle of Man TTs, which then counted for the world championships.

Within only two or three years of a modest debut they had achieved their initial goal of annihilating the reigning European lightweights (at that time 125 and 250 cc MV Agustas) through the simple logic of resurrecting paired valves, slashing cylinder size and exploiting new levels of engine speed.

But the very success of their bid saddled Honda with the much more formidable task of upholding four-stroke technology as a whole against the dawning two-stroke challenge. For the apparent dominance of the little double-knocker MVs had tended to conceal the brilliant development work of MZ's Walter Kaaden in East Germany, handicapped though he was by a pitiful shortage of resources and hard currency.

Scintillating performances in the late 1950s and early 1960s by Horst Fügner, Ernst Degner, Luigi Taveri and Gary Hocking had shown the disc-valve MZ two-strokes to be potential world champions in both the lightweight classes. And once Suzuki successfully tempted Degner to Japan with MZ's secrets, the two-stroke acquired what it had lacked in East Germany – the resources to back Kaaden's pioneering ideas.

First Suzuki then Yamaha mounted the two-stroke onslaught. But Honda – intensely proud of their newly won prestige – vigorously countered every move, cutting cylinder size progressively to 25 cc (50 cc twins and 125 cc fives) and boosting usable engine speed as high as 20,000 rpm.

Subsequent events make it doubtful whether Honda, at that stage, appreciated the inevitability of an ultimate two-stroke takeover, given the FIM formula of fixed engine capacities and no supercharging. Certainly they kept the four-stroke end up well enough to collar all five manufacturers' titles as late as 1966. So far as their hordes of supporters were concerned, the warning writing on the wall was too faint to be legible. Only those who had taken the trouble over the years to calculate the relative bhp/litre/1,000 rpm of the top engines of both types drew the inescapable conclusion that the grand-prix four-stroke's days were numbered.

Even so, the four-stroke would most likely have held sway a little longer if Honda had not quit the grands prix (along with Suzuki) at the end of 1967, leaving the two-stroke Yamahas to win the technical war by default.

Two-stroke technology maintained its momentum and when Honda decided to re-enter the grand-prix fray some 12 years later, their blind faith in the four-stroke's superiority, boosted by their lingering pride, precipitated a downfall that stunned their followers.

Heedless of a decade of runaway development in two-stroke track performance, they continued to hitch their wagon to the four-stroke star and set a team of fresh young engineers to design a 'world-beating' 500 cc four almost regardless of cost. Amazingly, the engineers came up with a 242-lb (110-kg) bike comprising a light-alloy monocoque chassis housing a 20,000 rpm, 100-degree V4 engine with a stroke of only 36 mm, four twin-choke carburettors and – most surprising of all – cylinders that, in plan view, were shaped like a running track (ie, an oval with the sides flattened). Each cylinder contained eight valves and two sparking plugs (two four-valve clusters, each with a central plug) and there were two connecting rods per piston.

Bold though the NR500 project undoubtedly was, the bike was outclassed on the track and, in three successive seasons, never finished in the top ten in a world-championship race. Eventually – while claiming that the research involved had helped in the development of their V4 roadsters – Honda tacitly conceded the two-stroke's superiority for world-championship racing: substituting a three-cylinder, reed-valve two-stroke for the 32-valver in 1982, they not only regained their

competitiveness almost immediately but started 1983 by repeatedly trouncing their rivals.

That, then, is a brief overall summary of Honda's grand-prix efforts. What of the details? Unafraid to plunge in at the deep end, they chose the TT for their European debut – the 1959 Lightweight 125 cc event over ten laps of the 10.79-mile (17.36-km) Clypse circuit. It was there that amused Western observers got their first glimpse of a routine that was to become familiar as other Japanese teams trod in Honda's footsteps – that of an advance party of camera-clicking little men assiduously committing to film anything and everything that might further their cause.

Equally amusing in European eyes was the quaint appearance of the ungainly little six-speed Honda parallel twins. Their excessively curved spine frames, long leading-link front forks and wet sumps made them uncommonly high for lightweights while the use of a larger wheel at the front than the rear dated their style considerably. Some engines had two-valve heads, some four. And although they peaked at a very brisk 13,000 rpm, their 18 bhp, along with the rawness of their home-bred riders, ruled out a competitive showing. Nevertheless, they were paragons of reliability and collared the manufacturers' team prize with sixth, seventh and eighth places.

For the same event the following year (1960, when the 37.73-mile Mountain lap was used) they had telescopic forks, same-size wheels and only the four-valve heads (with the cylinders inclined well forward to cool the central plugs without the air scoops used earlier). But although they filled sixth to tenth places inclusive, they failed to retain the team prize – and their fastest finisher, Naomi Taniguchi, was 5.52 mph (8.88 kph) slower than Carlo Ubbiali on the winning MV Agusta single.

However, their debut in the Lightweight 250 cc race, with a trio of impressive-looking, if bulky, fours, was more auspicious. Although the riders complained that engine power was apt to fluctuate spasmodically at top speed, the bikes were reliable and fast enough to finish fourth, fifth and sixth, albeit Australian Bob Brown (their best finisher) was 4.43 mph (7.13 kph) slower than Gary Hocking, who won on an MV twin.

A clue to their reliability was given when the Honda technicians confided that each valve weighed only 12 grammes and that its total reciprocating weight, including cam follower, duplex springs and top collar, was 20 grammes (well under 0.75 oz). By this means maximum safe revs were pushed as high as 17,000 rpm – 3,500 beyond the peak-power level, at which 38 bhp was claimed.

Developments during the year boosted peak power to 40 bhp for the four and 20 for the twin, while the frame was changed to a duplex structure attached to the stressed power unit at the cylinder head and gearbox, with the top and down tubes crossed over behind the steering head to reduce height.

No less important, the team's riding strength was deepened by adding Rhodesian Jim Redman (who eventually won six TTs and six world titles for Honda) to the Australian pair of Brown and Tom Phillis. True, the top Italian lightweights continued to trounce the Hondas in the season's

Partially dismantled at Honda's Nursery Hotel depot in Onchan in 1959, this early 125 cc parallel twin looks ungainly with its high tank, curved frame spine and spindly front fork. Camshaft drive to the two-valve heads is by shaft and bevels

Above: original top-heavy 250 cc four, with knobbly front tyre, as raced on rough mountain tracks at Asama Plains, Japan, in 1959. A much modified version made its TT debut the following year

Right: by the time it was brought to Europe for the TT in 1960, the 250 cc four had the cylinders inclined forward, the camshafts driven by a central gear train (not shaft and bevels), a telescopic front fork and a ribbed front tyre

remaining grands prix but the Japanese engineers had a solid base to build on during the 1960-61 winter.

And build they certainly did, improving both carburation and ignition to sort out the engines' tantrums, increasing power by five per cent, uniting the fairing sides in a smooth underbelly and boosting riding strength still further by engaging the up-and-coming Mike Hailwood, the dapper little Swiss star, Luigi Taveri, and the most dynamic TT rider of them all – Bob McIntyre.

The net result, in both Lightweight races, was nothing short of massacre, with Hondas filling the first five places. Although Hailwood won them both and Taveri upped Ubbiali's 125 cc lap record by a cool 2.35 mph (to 88.45), the sensation of the week was McIntyre's superhuman performance in the 250 cc race. Despite a liberal oil leak on to the rear tyre (a problem he had struggled with throughout practice) he lapped at 99.58 mph (160.26 kph) – 4.11 mph faster than Ubbiali's lap record and 0.38 mph better than John Surtees' *350 cc* lap record, both set the previous year. But for his handicap, Mac would have been the first Lightweight rider to turn a 100 mph lap, a feat previously achieved only by himself, Surtees, John Hartle, Derek Minter and Hailwood on 500 cc machines.

The cause of McIntyre's trouble was the factory's change from wet-sump oiling to dry, to lower the engine. Whether the other team machines would have wilted in the same way under Mac's whip no-one knows. What is certain is that his prodigious mastery of the circuit's twists and turns subjected his engine to longer periods of full throttle than the others. Pumped around the system every half-minute, the half-gallon of oil had insufficient time to shed its surplus heat; as its temperature soared beyond 100 degrees C, it frothed hopelessly and seeped out of the tank to make left-hand cornering hazardous.

Except for those of us in the know, nobody would have suspected it, for even Mac's standing-start lap bit more than 48 seconds off Ubbiali's record and put the Scot nearly half a minute clear of the second man, Gary Hocking (MV).

Mac's brand-new record lasted only until he completed his second lap (his first flier), which not only whittled more than 10 seconds off it but also bettered Surtees' Junior record (on an MV four) by 5.4 seconds. On his third lap, McIntyre had only to shave 5.8 seconds off his second-lap time to put the howling little Honda in the ton-lap club.

But it was not to be. More and more, the oil on the left side of the rear tyre curbed his cornering style – albeit his lead was so handsome that only the cruellest luck could rob him of victory. That it did on the very last lap, when the oil tank ran dry and the engine seized at the Quarry bends. For Honda, however, the blow was softened as Hailwood gratefully accepted McIntyre's gift of the race, followed home by his team-mates, Phillis and Redman.

As the season rolled on, engine developments steadily boosted power while weight was kept in check (the two-fifty scaled in at only 231 lb) and it was no surprise that Hailwood (250 cc) and Phillis (125 cc) won the world lightweight championships, so putting an end to Ubbiali's long run of titles for MV.

Thus encouraged, Honda broadened their effort in 1962 to embrace both the 350 and the new 50 cc classes. The tiddler was virtually an undersize half of the 125 cc twin, with the double overhead camshafts similarly driven by a long train of gears, while the 350 cc contender was, at first, simply a two-fifty bored out to 285 cc.

Appropriately, the little single was ridden by the team's dwarfs – Luigi Taveri and Irish Tommy Robb. Despite their prowess, however, and the bike's skinny proportions and 132 lb (60 kg) weight, its 9 bhp at 14,000 rpm was no match for the 10 bhp at 11,000 rpm and superior torque of Ernst Degner's two-stroke Suzuki; in 50 cc racing a small difference in power can make a big difference to race speed because the engine spends so much time on full throttle. It was Degner who won the TT handsomely, likewise the world championship.

Initially, the 285 cc four also seemed unlikely to worry the opposition – Hailwood and Hocking on

A paddock scene from the Dutch Grand Prix at Assen in 1961, the year Honda riders won their first world championships – Tom Phillis 125 cc, Mike Hailwood 250 cc. In the middle of the standing group (wearing hat and facing camera) is Mike's father, Stan

MV fours – for both McIntyre and Phillis broke down in the Junior TT. But the engineers quickly chased the bugs away for Jim Redman to get the MVs' measure. Towards the end of the season, engine capacity was boosted by 54 cc to 339 cc (49 × 45 mm); and when the new motor made its debut in the Ulster Grand Prix the Rhodesian romped to an emphatic win, thereby clinching the 350 cc title that MV had monoplised for the previous four years.

In their established classes (125 cc and 250 cc) there was never any doubt of Honda maintaining their superiority. With an extra bhp or two to play with, the twins retained their clock-like regularity to fill the first five places again in the Isle of Man – and Taveri, the winner and lap record breaker, kept up his scintillating form throughout the year to head Redman and Robb at the top of the world-championship table.

The 250 cc four, too, had gained a few bhp during the preceding winter, though at the cost of an elusive misfire that took some of the shine off its phenomenal reputation for reliability. Although their rivals would have been glad to match them, filling only the first three places in the TT seemed a bit of a comedown for Honda, especially as the winning speed was 1.7 mph slower than in 1961.

But there was no sign of decline when the race got under way – quite the contrary. McIntyre was again hot favourite. With the relief of a dry rear tyre, he romped round at 99.06 mph (159.42 kph) from a standing start (an improvement of 3.2 seconds over 1961) and established a stupendous lead of 34.6 seconds over the next man, Redman, and 44 seconds over Derek Minter, the eventual winner. This time, surely, fate would not rob the Scot and his Honda of the first 250 cc ton lap.

Not only Honda supporters but everyone around the course was ready to cheer at the expected announcement. The 14,000 rpm symphony from the four long megaphones was as sweet and haunting as ever. Alas, on the ultrafast swoop to Baaregarroo, only 12 miles out, it suddenly collapsed to a stutter as two cylinders lost their sparks.

Even Minter's victory was not undiluted joy for the official team, for he was riding a spare machine borrowed from the UK importers (Hondis) and was not supposed to beat Redman and Phillis as he did! In the season as a whole, however, these were small hiccups, for Redman bagged the 250 cc championship (followed by McIntyre), so bringing Honda's tally of individual titles to three for the year.

In 1963 Honda learned that there is nothing permanent about invincibility. They had yet to make their mark in the 50 cc class. Indeed, so uncompetitive had their first tiddler been in 1962 – when Taveri was beaten in the title chase not only by Degner on the Suzuki but also by Hans-Georg Anscheidt on a 12-speed Kreidler – that they decided not to contest the class for a year, so giving the engineers time to come up with something entirely new.

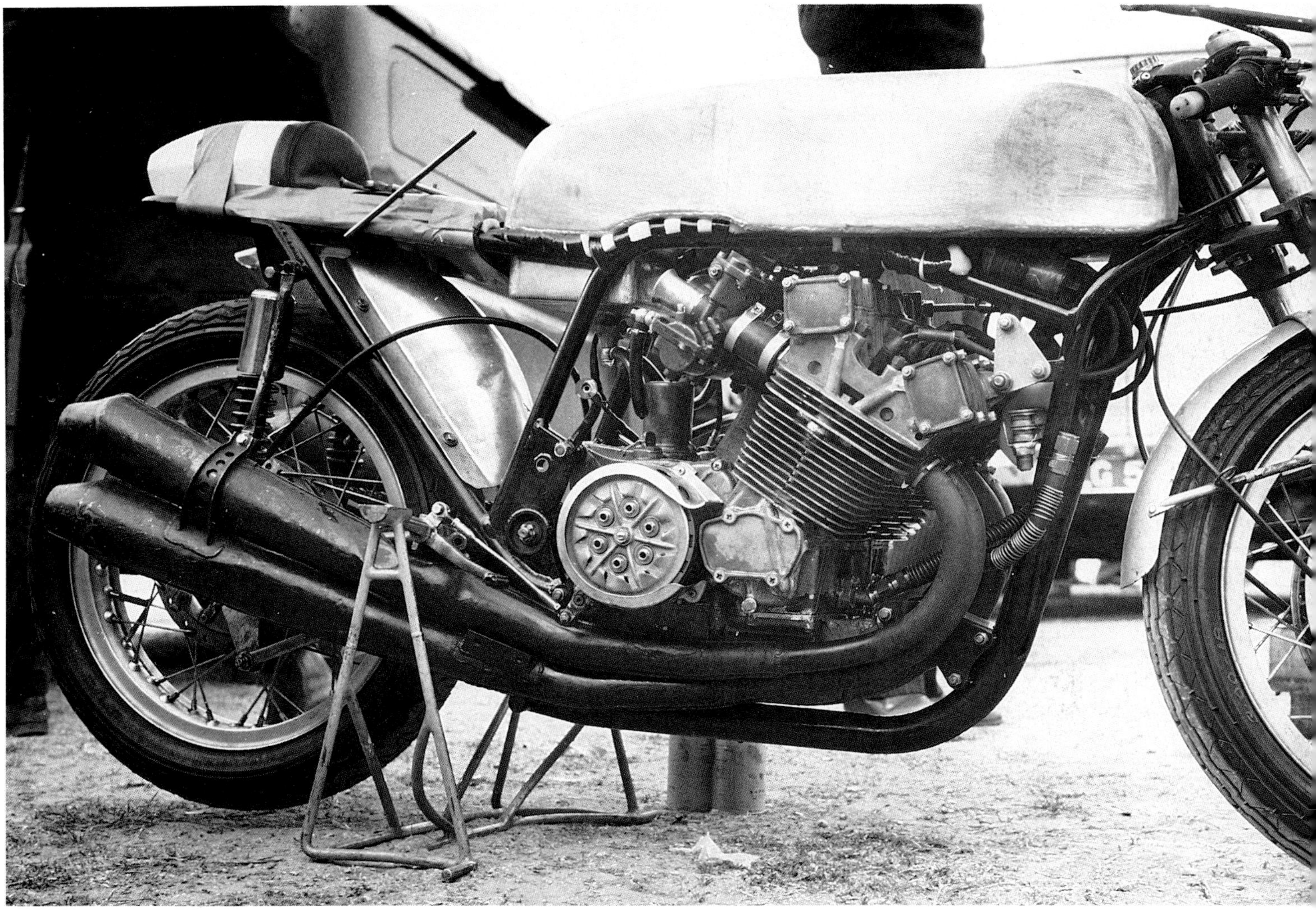

An unexpected drubbing in the 125 cc class – by a team of Suzuki air-cooled twins, spearheaded by New Zealander Hugh Anderson – then convinced Honda that they must go back to the drawing board in that category too.

Dependable Jim Redman managed to hang on to his 250 and 350 cc titles, but it was a close-run thing in the smaller class. The first fright was administered in the TT, by Fumio Ito on a Yamaha air-cooled twin. For the first two laps the tearaway Japanese led the world champion; and although Redman moved ahead when Ito made an appallingly indifferent pit stop, the Yamaha man chased him home to the finish – a performance he repeated in Holland and Japan and improved on by winning in Belgium.

MZ riders also revealed the Honda four's vulnerability to the two-stroke challenge when Hailwood won at Sachsenring on a water-cooled twin, and when Alan Shepherd's winning potential at Hockenheim and Monza was discounted only by early pit stops. But the most consistent threat in 1963, in defiance of the overall technical trend, came from the fiery Tarquinio Provini on the double-knocker Moto Morini single. With

Above: *the promised 500 cc four with which Honda tempted Mike Hailwood back from the MV Agusta camp in 1966. Although difficult to handle, it took him to an emphatic victory in the Senior TT, nearly three minutes ahead of Giacomo Agostini on a 12-valve MV three*

Left: *in the Hockenheim paddock at the 1963 West German Grand Prix, Honda stars Jim Redman (helmeted) and Luigi Taveri compare notes. The Rhodesian amassed six world titles for Honda, the Swiss three*

With both four and six cylinders, Honda proved that stretching a successful 250 cc engine is a first-class recipe for a world-beating three-fifty. Here is the four, which started at 285 cc in 1962, then grew to 339 cc (see here in 1963) and finally to 349 cc in 1964. Ridden by Jim Redman, it won the world championship in each of those years and in 1965

spectacular wins at Montjuich Park, Hockenheim and Monza, he kept the issue wide open until the final round, in Japan, where to Honda's great relief, Redman won.

What little peace of mind Honda enjoyed throughout 1963 came from the 350 cc class, where Hailwood's eight-valve MV – virtually an underpowered five-hundred and long-in-the-tooth at that – was no match for an up-to-date 16-valve bike that was essentially an overpowered two-fifty. In desperation, MV concocted an enormous twin-leading-shoe front brake for Hailwood, in the hope that he might offset the Honda's superior speed and acceleration in the TT by later braking. Mike tried his utmost but wore out the massive brake in a vain bid to hold the Honda before being forced to retire. By the end of the year Redman had a comfortable four points in hand for the title.

For the first time since they stunned the racing world, Honda had their backs to the wall. It was clear that the best disc-valve two-strokes had a significant advantage in bhp/litre/1000 rpm, so Honda took the only course available within the FIM rules – which was to cut cylinder size and so push up peak revs beyond the level to which the two-strokes were limited by their scanty lubrication.

For their re-entry into the 50 cc fray, they produced a tiny parallel twin that had a technical fascination out of all proportion to its size. The engine was virtually a miniaturised version of one of the fours with the offside two cylinders cut off, so that the camshaft gear train was on the right; the crankshaft, too, resembled the left half of a four, with the crankpins spaced at 180 degrees so that the pistons moved in opposite directions.

Those pistons would easily have dropped into liqueur glasses, for bore and stroke were 33 × 29.2 mm, while the valve heads were about half an inch across and the plugs only 10 mm in diameter. Astonishingly, the engine turned over at 19,000 rpm to produce its 15 bhp, was mechanically safe beyond 20,000 rpm and required nine speeds to keep it on the boil.

No less novel was the rest of the bike. In keeping the weight down to within 4 lb (1.82 kg) of that of the original single, Honda fitted a cycle-type caliper front brake acting on the wheel rim, and tyres of only 2.00 and 2.25 inches in section. Fairing width was minimised by crossing the exhaust pipes over in front of the cylinder head; and although the handlebar complied with the FIM minimum-width requirement of 18 inches, the grips were mounted well inboard to keep the rider's arms out of the airstream. Drag was further reduced by clipping light-alloy streamline discs to the spokes on both sides, although the front discs were removed for gusty conditions.

Debugging the little screamer took half the season, during which Suzuki star Hugh Anderson led Bryans home in the TT, then quickly amassed enough points to retain his world championship. But in narrowing the points gap by the end of the year with four consecutive victories, the Irishman finished on the crest of a wave and sent Suzuki scurrying back to *their* drawing board. They also went to two cylinders – water cooling too – but the little Honda's momen-

tum carried it through 1965, when both Bryans and Taveri pushed Anderson off his title perch.

Back in 1964, the other brand-new Honda to emerge from the race shop was a 125 cc four to replace the beaten twin. This time there were no bugs – seemingly they switched their attention to Suzuki, robbing them of reliability in exchange for a bit more speed. With 25 bhp at 16,000 rpm and eight speeds, the new Honda had speed enough for Taveri to stick 2 to 3 mph on the TT lap and race records (backed up by Redman and Bryans in the next two places) – and dependability enough for him to notch five wins and four second spots in regaining the world title, with Redman also heading Anderson.

If that result seemed to fend off the two-stroke challenge, it was otherwise in the 250 cc class, where Phil Read's air-cooled Yamaha twin was a veritable flier. True it lacked the stamina for the TT course, where Read broke down, leaving Redman to win, but nearly everywhere else Read was able to tease the Rhodesian by shadowing him throughout the race and romping by to win in the closing stages. Jim's and Honda's consolation came from the ease with which he brought his tally of 350 cc titles up to three on the trot, winning every grand prix in the series, with the engine finally stretched to full size (349 cc) by a slight flattening of the cylinder dimensions to 50 × 44.5 mm.

In 1965 Honda's joy was confined to Ralph Bryans' world 50 cc championship already mentioned and Redman's fourth (and last) 350 cc title. In that class, MV had belatedly responded to the Japanese takeover with a 12-valve three-cylinder engine that simultaneously narrowed the bike and boosted its power. But, exuberantly though Giacomo Agostini rode it, the Italian machine was down on Honda power and Redman had a comfortable six points in hand at the finish.

Things were far from rosy in the 125 and 250 cc classes, however, where the factory's efforts in Formula 1 car racing diluted their concentration and machine preparation suffered. Taveri's one-two-five, such a honey in 1964, refused to fire cleanly for the first half of the season. Meanwhile, Yamaha and Suzuki had gained both power and stamina from water cooling their little twins, with the result that Read beat Taveri in the TT and Anderson emphatically regained his world title.

Honda's disappointment galvanised them into swift action. Taking advantage of the success of Bryans' 50 cc twin, they clapped five of the tiny cylinders on a common crankcase and wheeled out the new bike for the season's final grand prix, in Japan. There, with 30 bhp on tap at 18-19,000 rpm and a top whack of 125 mph, Taveri and Bryans had the legs of everyone else in the race and only a trivial fault robbed Taveri of victory. Clearly, firm foundations were laid for 1966.

Something similar had happened a year earlier in the 250 cc class. Annoyed at the ease with which Read had been able to toy with Redman for most of the season, Honda had fielded a masterpiece of miniaturisation at Monza – a six instead of a four. It was not an instant success; Redman found it a bit of a camel and misfiring as well. He finished third. By the time of the Japa-

After being dethroned by Hugh Anderson (Suzuki) in the 1963 world 125 cc championship, Luigi Taveri was given this brand-new, eight-speed four in place of his ageing twin and regained the title for Honda the following year

nese GP, however, the engine at least had been sorted and Jim was uncatchable.

It seemed that 1965 would find Honda back on top of the 250 cc heap. Unhappily for them, Redman struck a bad patch while Read was still riding high. The six contined to be a handful and suffered mechanical failures too. When Read's Yamaha crankshaft broke in the Island, Jim went on to win his third successive Lightweight 250 cc TT but Phil then demoralised the Honda camp with four straight wins on less demanding circuits. Redman had two other successes – in Belgium and Czechoslovakia – but since he made only six starts throughout the season to Read's 12, Phil had no difficulty in piling on three more wins to retain his title in resounding fashion.

Realising that the loyal Redman was approaching the end of his tether anyway, Honda made further use of the year's last meeting at Suzuka by offering the younger Hailwood a ride on the six. Mike's blunt criticism of its handling made the Japanese headlines; but four years' experience of the heavier MVs stood him in good stead and he gave the opposition no chance. Honda put him on the payroll and their prospects for 1966 looked brighter still, especially as they provided him with a five-hundred. . . .

Mike's comprehensive experience soon helped sort out the two-fifty's handling – after which his incomparable riding, allied to the bike's astonishing slimness (no wider across the fairing than a single), dependability and stronger engine braking, gave Read no chance of retaining the championship, notwithstanding his switch from the air-cooled Yamaha twin to a V4 based on their successful air-cooled 125 cc twin.

Indeed, in allowing Mike to rattle up ten 250 cc victories when seven would have sufficed for the title, Honda scuppered his chance of winning the 500 cc championship too. With 85 bhp at 12,000 rpm, the big new 16-valve four was more than a match for Agostini's old eight-valve MV four – and even for the 12-valve three they subsequently gave him by stretching the three-fifty first to 420 then to 489 cc.

Mike's 2 minutes 37.8 seconds beating of Ago in the Senior TT made it plain that the title was his for the taking. But Honda chose to reward Redman's loyalty by letting him shoulder the five-hundred's hopes, believing that its surplus power would more than offset Agostini's extra dash. Redman won at Hockenheim and Assen, although his margin over the Italian in Holland was very slender. But when Jim broke an arm at Francorchamps the following week his points became irrelevant, except for the manufacturers' contest. Had Mike Hailwood been selected for the German and Dutch victories, the individual title would have been a doddle for him. Even as it was, Mike still had the championship within his grasp at Monza when the crankshaft failed, landing the title in Ago's grateful lap and sending the partisan crowd wild with delight.

To counter the growing threat from Agostini's 12-valve three in the 350 cc division, Honda laid the old four to rest and stretched the capacity of the exciting new six to the limit – 297 cc. It was more than enough. Hailwood scored six impressive wins and the only times Agostini beat him were when Mike retired – in the Island and on the Sachsenring. The Italian also won before his home crowd at Monza – where, with the title already in the bag, Mike was a non-starter.

In the 50 cc class, too, Honda took a decision that made the opposition a gift of the individual world championship. In the TT, both Bryans and Taveri (in that order) had relegated Anderson to third place – and throughout the season the Honda duo maintained a confident edge. But when the final round, in Japan, was moved from its customary venue at Suzuka (Honda's test track) the team boycotted the event in protest. In their absence, Anscheidt enjoyed an untroubled win for Suzuki, thereby turning a six-point deficit into a two-point advantage to notch the first of his three consecutive titles in the class.

The 125 cc contest started badly for Honda when all their TT entries were slowed by faulty carburation, leaving Bill Ivy and Read to fill the first two places on their Yamaha twins. But the five-cylinder engine soon got into its stride and, with typical determination, Taveri finished the season with five wins to Ivy's four and so clinched his third title in the class within five years.

Honda's clean sweep of all five manufacturers' championships in 1966 reflected great strength in depth and it is sometimes argued that these titles are a truer measure of technical merit than are the individual titles. But try telling that to the fans whose allegiance in the market place is determined by world championship results. To a man, they are more influenced by the glamour of the individual titles – therefore Honda would have done better to give priority to Mike Hailwood's chances in the 500 cc contest and Taveri's and Bryans' in the tiddler class.

By 1967 it was clear to the Honda race engi-

One of Honda's most successful grand-prix engines, the remarkably narrow transverse straight-six started life as a two-fifty late in 1964 and was subsequently bored and stroked to 297 cc. It powered Mike Hailwood to both 250 and 350 world championships in 1966 and 1967

Opposite, top: *Toppled off their 125 cc perch again in 1965, Honda introduced this five-cylinder version (based on the 50 cc twin) in the Japanese Grand Prix in October and Taveri regained the title in 1966. Note the cunning way of accommodating the middle exhaust pipe*

Opposite, bottom: *introduced in 1964 and ridden to the world championship by Ralph Bryans the following year – the featherweight, nine-speed 50 cc twin. Downswept exhausts are fitted here, although a high-level crossover layout was also used. Front brake is caliper type, working on the wheel rim. Thin aluminium discs were clipped to the spokes to smooth the airflow.*

Honda's first two road racing stars, Australian Tom Phillis (left) and South African Jim Redman photographed at the 1961 Italian GP at Monza

neers that the two-stroke/four-stroke struggle was approaching a climax, at least in the smallest three classes if not yet in the 350 and 500 cc divisions.

It was true that the track performance of the more powerful Yamaha 250 cc V4 was at that stage still blunted, especially in the Isle of Man, by its untamed handling (although Read eventually ran Hailwood close in the championship). But the 50 cc bike needed more power if it was to stay ahead of the Suzukis – and so did the one-two-five now that Yamaha had scaled down their V4 for that class and Suzuki had a similar machine under test.

So Honda withdrew from 50 and 125 cc racing to concentrate on new designs – a three-cylinder tiddler and maybe a scaled-down version of the six – little suspecting they would never be ridden in anger, for the management were to call a halt to the grand-prix programme at the end of the year.

While Anscheidt took advantage of Honda's absence to retain his 50 cc crown (backed up by his team-mates Yosh Katayama and Stuart Graham) and Bill Ivy covered himself in glory while romping to a 16-point margin in the 125 cc chase, Hailwood more than justified his contract in the other three classes. He won all three of his TT races – the Lightweight 250 cc and Junior by enormous margins, and the Senior after a titanic struggle not only with Agostini but also with a loose twistgrip that aggravated the big Honda's bad handling. Overall, he retained his 250 and 350 cc championships but Agostini again won the 500 cc category, although both finished on 46 points.

Honda's unexpected withdrawal from this, the purest form of racing was widely regretted. Technically, it brought to an end one of the most colourful eras in the history of the world championships – and that at a time when it seemed the curtain was about to rise on the final thrilling act in the two-stroke/four-stroke confrontation. It is true that Suzuki pulled out at the same time; but that still left Yamaha, already the chief protagonist, to carry the two-stroke banner. For the four-stroke, the only really serious contender left in the solo classes was MV – and the Italian team, if only because of its relatively slender resources, could not hope to take over Honda's dynamic role.

During the 12 years that elapsed before Honda sought to regain their former glory on the grand-prix scene, the two-stroke made prodigious strides, conquering not only all five solo classes but the sidecars too. Its inherent advantage in weight had been reinforced by greatly enhanced reliability. Most important of all – especially considering the unprecedented levels of grip the tyre boffins had meanwhile provided – it had opened up a gap in specific power (bhp/litre) that seemed totally unrealistic for anyone to expect to close with a poppet valve four-stroke.

In terms of bhp/litre/1000 rpm (a useful yardstick here) the top two-stroke engines were already approaching 25 with no sign of a full stop. By comparison, the best unblown four-strokes (including Honda's earlier grand-prix engines and even the remarkably efficient 3-litre Cosworth-Ford Formula 1 car engine) had long been stuck around 15, with no sign of a breakthrough. Honda planned to get on terms with the best two-strokes by matching their efficiency for each complete engine cycle (two revolutions for Honda, one for the two-stroke) at twice the two-stroke's crankshaft speed – i.e., some 22,000 rpm.

While it made sense to choose the 500 cc class, where the premium on sheer power is not so overwhelming as in the smaller classes, that choice limited them to four cylinders – a ceiling imposed by the FIM since Honda's withdrawal. And, for cylinders of 125 cc, 22,000 rpm was so far along the path of diminishing returns that any potential power gains would long since have been overtaken by friction and pumping losses, besides breathing difficulties.

To keep the valves under control – and in the hope of maintaining deep breathing – Honda put four tiny inlet valves and four exhausts in parallel rows in each cylinder; hence the 'oval' bores, twin-choke carburettors and double con-rods to prevent the pistons from tilting. The combustion chambers were anything but compact; and though twin plugs shortened the flame travel, the surface area absorbing otherwise-useful heat was uncommonly large. Moreover, since valve timings are essentially time-based, the proposed engine speed stretched the angular timings so much that both inlet and exhaust valves were well off their seats at top dead centre overlap, so restricting piston-crown height, hence compression ratio.

The two-stroke three-cylinder NS500 that gave Honda their first grand prix success for 15 years when Freddie Spencer won the 1982 Belgium Grand Prix at Spa

At best, this venture into unexplored realms of four-stroke technology could be seen as a heroic gamble. But highly qualified engineers of wide experience were apt to regard it as a futile attempt by a team of young greenhorns to make monkeys of the world's best four-stroke brains.

Honda's strategy for the chassis – light, slim and slippery to minimise the power requirement – also made sense on paper. But in practice its unorthodox detail design and 16 inch wheels proved unsatisfactory. On its Silverstone debut in the 1979 British GP and later in the French GP at Le Mans, the NR500 was hopelessly off the pace. The engine was difficult to start, tricky to control, thirsty and underpowered, while the suddenness with which it stopped when shut off told of high internal friction. Accessibility and handling were both bad. Even dynamometer results were inconsistent; seizures were frequent.

The monocoque chassis was discarded in favour of a British-designed tubular frame. Minor engine changes were made, though nothing fundamental. But still the results did not come. Within two years of the NR500's debut, Honda conceded the invincibility of the two-stroke under the FIM's grand-prix engine formula and designed a three-cylinder two-stroke – the NS500 – for 1982.

The 1981 world champion, Marco Lucchinelli, and the brilliant young American Freddie Spencer were signed to race it.

Since the new engine inherited reed-valve induction from the factory's moto-crossers, it was thought to be a stop-gap while the engineers perfected a disc-valve square four. But, with two cylinders upright and one prone, the new bike was admirably compact and handled well. To Honda's immense relief, their technical prowess was vindicated when Takazumi Katayama won the Swedish GP at Anderstorp on the NS500 and Freddie Spencer rode it to victory in the Belgian GP at Francorchamps and the San Marino GP at Mugello.

If the opposition regarded those late-season victories as some sort of flash in the pan they were soon disillusioned. The 1983 season opened (in South Africa) with Kenny Roberts as determined as only he can be to add a fourth world 500 cc title to his 1978-79-80 hat-trick for Yamaha before quitting the classic scene at the end of the year. Suzuki, meanwhile, were quietly confident of maintaining the dominance that had brought them the last two titles, through Lucchinelli and Franco Uncini. Yet Honda stole the limelight right from the start.

With an organisation that threatened to bankrupt Japan (to quote *Motor Cycle Weekly* reporter Nick Harris) they arrived at Kyalami with two bikes for each rider, five technicians for each bike and a trio of bouncers and guard dogs to boot. But it was on the track that they made the greatest impression – for Spencer decisively beat Roberts, while Honda new boy Ron Haslam took third place. At Le Mans two weeks later they did even better, taking the first three places, with Lucchinelli sandwiched between winner Spencer and Haslam, and Roberts relegated to fourth place. Then, in the Italian GP at Monza, Spencer completed his hat-trick.

At the time of writing the 1983 title chase had a long way to run. But, whatever the eventual outcome might be, Honda had already shown quite clearly that the NR500 failure was due not to any lack of engineering talent but to an over-ambitious management bid to push the unblown four-stroke engine beyond its inherent limits.

Moto Cross

Although Honda was the first of the big Japanese bike manufacturers to go grand prix road racing, they were the last to enter the rough, tough arena of world championship moto cross. Their first year of grand prix moto cross competition came in 1975, and then it was very much a low-key, 'toe-in-the-water' exercise organised by their American organised by their American subsidiary.

Today, Honda's achievements in grand prix moto cross are well-known, especially in Great Britain, for it was a young Hampshire rider, Graham Noyce, who brought them their first world moto cross title in 1979.

But in Honda's 1975 debut, the factory left the team selection and organisation to American Honda who picked two very different riders – neither of whom were considered potential world champions at the time: young Californian Marty Smith and expatriate Dutchman Pierre Karsmakers. The plan was that Smith, 1974 US 125 National Champion, would try just the US round of the 125 cc FIM cup series while Karsmakers would take on the 500 cc boys over in Europe. It was very much a low-key start ... in sharp contrast to Honda's blitz on the world road racing championships back in 1960.

Honda were up against other Japanese bike makers, notably Suzuki whose achievements in grand prix moto cross can be compared with Honda's in road racing. By the start of the 1975 season Suzuki had already completed a grand slam of moto cross titles and in Belgians Joel Robert and Roger De Coster they had signed two men with proven and unrivalled moto cross abilities. Robert got Suzuki five world 250 cc titles on their quick and ultra-light machines and De Coster gave them three 500 cc titles.

Japanese rivals Yamaha had collected a 250 cc title with their new bike featuring a revolutionary monoshock rear suspension system and Kawasaki were beginning to get established in the 250 cc class with Swedes Torlief Hansen and Olle Petersson ... so new boys Honda were really up against some formidable opposition. So why, after a full-scale, large-budget blitz on the road racing world back in 1960 did Honda wait until

Honda's first moto cross machine – the 250 cc two-stroke single code-named 335C pictured in 1972

1975 to get into GP moto cross?

The chief reason for the delay was commercial. Honda went GP road racing to establish their name worldwide and open up overseas export markets. In 1967 their name was well-established so they pulled out of road racing – there was just no need to get into GP moto cross. At that time Honda manufactured no competition off-road machines or proper trail bikes so what could they gain by going into off-road competition?

Those years must have been frustrating for the motor cycle-mad men at Honda and those frustrations must have led to pressure for a return to some kind of motor cycle competition ... even moto cross. Equally it was commercial pressures that prompted Honda's entry into the moto cross game ... plus a little arm-twisting from Honda America.

The vast American off-road and moto cross bike market was largely virgin territory in the early 1970s with only Suzuki really getting stuck in there. Obviously Honda America were desperately anxious for the factory to come up with a serious dirt machine so that they could begin to win themselves a slice of the US off-road action, and at every opportunity they sold their message to the parent company in Japan.

Honda must have spotted the potential earlier themselves, of course, but they had their hands full simply meeting the vast worldwide demand for their bikes.

There is another reason, however: Honda's commitment to four-stroke machinery. Ever since those early immediate post-war Dream road machines all Hondas had a four-stroke power plant – a policy established by Soichiro Honda himself and well-understood by all Honda personnel. Soichiro had actually gone on record with the statement that: 'Honda will never build a two-stroke.'

In 1975 it must have been obvious to everyone that a four-stroke-only edict would just not work in moto cross – one had only to look at the runaway success Suzuki were enjoying. As early as the late 1960s the once-mighty British BSA moto cross team and their four-strokes had been toppled forever from their perch by the two-strokes, despite a last-minute massive investment in an ultra lightweight machine built largely of titanium and magnesium alloys.

But Soichiro Honda was the autocratic boss of the company he founded and it would not take a great leap of the imagination to picture him telling his R and D boffins that if they could not make a four-stroke that would be competitive with the Suzuki and Yamaha scramblers then Honda would not go moto cross racing.

Although there was never an official Honda four-stroke moto cross project, a handful of keen research engineers had for several years been racing a much-modified XL250 machine in races in Japan ... strictly as a private effort. Honda would not lend their name to this unofficial project but their established policy of encouraging individual talents in their research department meant that no one tried to interfere. However, the project was abandoned in 1971 when Honda finally recognised the need to have a scrambler in their range and officially formed the Moto Cross Machine Group within their own massive R and D organisation.

So there was never an official Honda four-stroke scrambler project – Honda really came into grand prix moto cross too late to make a thumper work seriously. Or did they? Just imagine, if history had dealt Honda a different hand and the Japanese giant had decided to go moto cross racing on their retirement from road racing ... would they have come up with a world-beating four-stroke? This is a fascinating prospect: in 1967 four-strokes could still win grand prix 500 cc events and with all the vast experience gained from their road-racing years and the immense talent and back-up of the R and D Department ... Honda would surely have been able to make a world-championship winning machine. If they had done that and kept at it we might not be faced with today's two-stroke domination of the moto cross championships.

The man who gets the credit for the Honda moto cross project is Soichiro Miyakoshi – then, in the late 1960s, a dead keen staff research engineer who had made a name for himself with his hand in the development, as a young man, of the grand prix four-stroke machines. Miyakoshi looked around at the off-road scene and at moto cross in particular and decided that two-strokes were the

Japanese works rider Taichi Yoshimura astride the first 250 cc machine in 1972. The man in the background is Mitsuoki Aika, now Managing Director of Honda Racing Corporation

BROC
YAMAHA
MOTO FOX
TOYOTA
HONDA
Kawasaki
11
9
154
63

HONDA
CR250M

Above: *Hondas at the front of the first turn – Americans Steve Wise (9) and Chuck Sun (63)*

Left: *the first production Honda moto crosser – the CR250M*

Right: *Brad Lackey leaps his big red Honda at the Swiss grand prix in 1979*

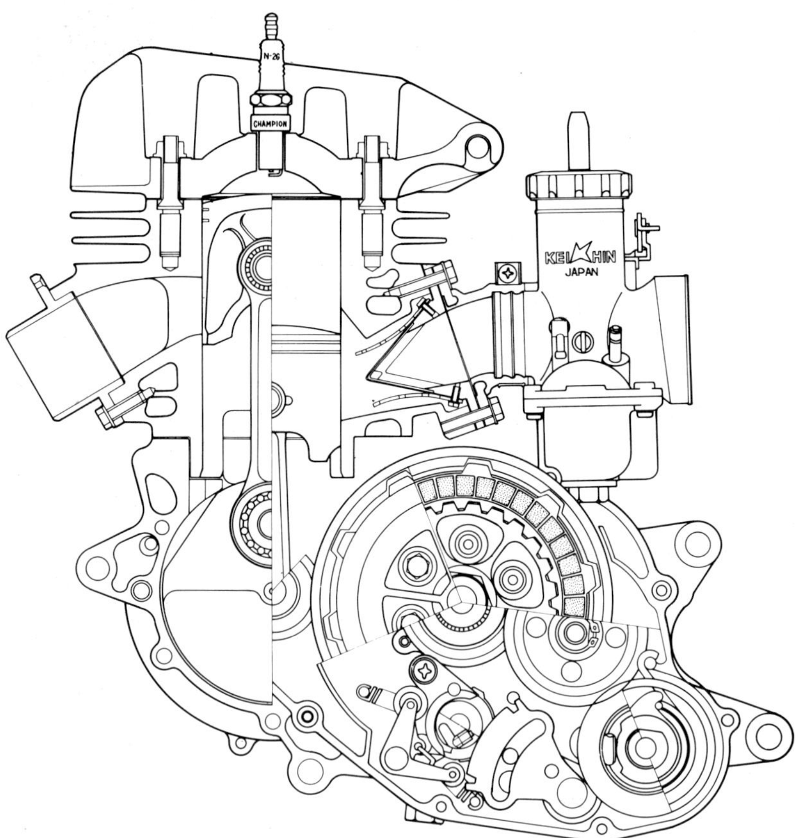

A part-section view of an early CR250 production moto cross engine – the latest version is water-cooled

way to go . . . four-stroke edict or not! With typical oriental thoroughness Miyakoshi applied his genius to the problem and literally taught himself everything there was to know about two-stroke technology. We can guess that the rival factory's machines were all methodically stripped down in his workshop, meticulously examined, measured and analysed.

Miyakoshi decided to apply two dictums that had given Honda success in road racing and Suzuki their moto cross victories – low weight and high power. In the winter of 1971 Honda had a compact, ultra-lightweight, and very potent 250 cc racer ready to race. Code named '335C' the machine had radical port timing but conventional oversquare bore and stroke dimensions of 70 × 64 mm. Coincidentally, perhaps, Soichiro Honda himself retired from heading the R and D Department personally in April of the same year.

The machine – without any giveaway Honda logo or gold wing on the tank – was raced several times in Japanese championship races in October, November and December 1971 without distinguishing itself. But by the time the machine was officially announced in February 1972, and riders Hirokazu Ueno and Taichi Yoshimura signed to contest national championship events, most of the bugs had been ironed out.

The first race with Yoshimura and Ueno was at Yatabe in the 250 cc All Japan moto cross event where the former came home sixth, the latter seventh. By this time the machines were officially designated RC250M. Incidentally one of the '335C' machines had been secretly shipped out to the USA late in 1971 for evaluation by the moto cross-mad men at Honda America.

In June 1972 a 125 cc machine – the RC125M – was announced and Yoshimura entered a works machine (code-named RC125M (AOF)) at Aomori, finishing fourth.

Honda had already established a precedent for light weight. Their '335C' machine reputedly weighed just 185 lb (84 kg) dry and produced around 30 bhp at the rear wheel – powerful for 1972. However, the 125 that Yoshimura raced at Aomori weighed just 154 lb (70 kg) dry – 22 lb below the new weight limit announced by the FIM to rule out expensive one-off factory specials in the grands prix. The bike developed 21 bhp at the rear wheel at 9,500 rpm making it very fast indeed.

Early in 1972 Honda finally admitted that they planned to go grand prix moto cross racing – perhaps in the 250 cc class in 1973.

It was in 1972 that the scene switched to the West Coast of the United States – to the American Honda Motor Co Incorporated at Gardena, California. There officials had been pressing for Honda to get involved in the off-road scene. As former American Honda moto cross manager Terry Mulligan explains: 'At that time, 1972, the off-road market was virtually untouched, though Yamaha and Suzuki were getting more serious and sales were starting to pick up. Pressure from our dealer network was increasing for a decent competitive off-road bike.' There had been plenty of contact between American Honda and Japan, and although they were never actually told – 'yes, we are building a 250 cc moto crosser' – no one at Gardena was surprised when the first works CR250 machine came over late in 1971.

Then things started to swing into action: Honda America signed up local southern California riders Jim Wilson and Bill Silverthorne under the team managership of John Blum. Wilson was a very experienced rider – in the late 1960s he had won the US Junior Trials Championship; when signed by Honda he was winning regularly on his British Greeves two-stroke. These two were not official riders and signed no formal contracts – they were freelance test riders for those early bikes.

The first works two-fiftys proved tremendously powerful – but were not tough enough to stand up to the beating they took on the fast, bone-hard Californian tracks. Honda America campaigned these bikes in local southern California events with Wilson and Silverthorne but the early races were something of a disappointment. Frames bent after 20 or 30 minutes and stones pierced the fuel tanks. Wheels broke and swing arms bent – clearly in their desire to produce an ultra-lightweight machine Honda had gone a little too far.

Honda had used a lot of their early road racing experience and despite the fact that these early bikes certainly were light – between 176 and 180 lb (80 kg) – they could not finish a full race intact. They are remembered at Honda America as being extremely fast – the fastest. But the frame geometry was clearly not right and the machine did not like corners. Initial work, after a stronger machine had been built, was aimed at

Opposite: *American teenage sensation Marty Smith in grand prix action on an early CR125 machine in 1976*

35

shortening the wheelbase and sorting out the front-end geometry.

Honda were eager to learn and after every race – and every breakage – a report was sent back to Japan; eventually the bikes went back too. By the end of the year the machines were much improved and the production CR250 machines that went on sale in the USA in the spring of 1973 were largely bug-free. Of course Honda did not have to make these machines ultra-light, but they were keen to sell the lightest production two-fifty, and with a claimed dry weight of just 214 lb (97 kg) the CR250 was just that.

Honda quickly followed up their moto cross machine with a trail version – the MT250. Mass production of the CR250 and a 125 cc version – the 125M – began in September 1972 and March 1973 respectively under the name Elsinore. Initially they were for the Japanese market with exports following a few months later. Honda called their early moto cross production machines Elsinore – not named after Hamlet's castle but after the American city where the cross country 'Elsinore grand prix' was held each year.

To cut the weight, extensive use was made of alloys. The frame, a conventional single down-tube semi-duplex type – was in a chrome-molybdenum alloy and the engine was all-aluminium with magnesium side covers. The cylinder barrel had a steel liner and six transfer ports, and a new style of combustion chamber to give improved scavenging. Claimed power for the CR250 was 33 bhp at 7,500 rpm with a maximum torque of 24 lb/ft at 6,500 rpm. A five-speed gearbox was fitted.

The front suspension gave 6.5 inches of movement, and the rear swing arm 4 inches. Seat height was 31 inches – Honda were keen that the machine should not be a handful. Early tests gave the ready to race weight with 1 gallon of fuel in the 1.5 gallon tank as 228 lb (103 kg). That first machine was green with a silver tank – it was not until 1974-5 that the distinctive 'fire-engine' red look was used.

For the 1973 season Honda signed the 1972 National 250 cc Champion Gary Jones, his brother Dwayne and two others: Marty Tripes and Bruce Barron. The Jones brothers and Tripes campaigned essentially stock machines, though by now a small development shop had been established, where parts were being modified and a certain amount of experiments carried out.

During the season Japan sent over a number of special parts for the Americans to race test: frames, swing arms, pistons, heads and barrels . . . all kinds of special equipment was being developed. Feedback was quick – the Americans invariably returned worn-out parts and the R and D response was fast: new or modified parts came over shortly after.

Gary Jones devoted his time to contesting the 250 cc National Championship and, although he raced both stock and works machinery, Honda America say that his eventual championship victory – his second in a row – was achieved mainly on stock CR250s.

Twice world champion – in 1981 and 1982 – Belgian André Malherbe in action

Another notable achievement in 1973 was Tripes' venture into the inter-AMA 250 cc international series. Tripes, who had finished in eighth place in the previous series on a Yamaha, finished sixth overall in the Honda's first-ever international competition. Later in 1973 Billy Grossi joined the Honda US team . . . not too late however to clinch third place in the national 250 cc class.

Grossi was the only man to stay with Honda for 1974 and new faces signed up were Marty Smith (a 17-years-old Californian), Bruce McDougal, Chuck Bower, and Mick Boone.

For 1974 Grossi stuck with the 250 cc class while the rest contested the brand-new 125 cc class. All riders spent most of their time on stock equipment, and by the end of the series Honda had finished a record breaking one, two, three and four in the 125 cc championship: Smith took the title followed by McDougal, Bower and Boone. Two more men (neither with official contracts), Jeff Foland and Dan Turner, finished up in seventh and eighth spots. That same year Honda entered Smith in the US round of the 125 cc 'grand prix' – actually known as the FIM Cup series before it was given world championship status in 1975. Smith achieved a respectable fourth place, gaining valuable 125 cc GP experience.

Anxious to get into the 500 cc class Honda signed up former Dutch and American champion Pierre Karsmakers from Yamaha in 1975. A man with a solid reputation as a top development rider, Karsmakers' brief was to get Honda established in open class competition. Smith re-signed to contest the 125 cc nationals for 1975 and Karsmakers was sent over to Europe to contest as many grands prix as his schedule would permit.

During his stay with Honda Karsmakers was built a bike that was fiercely powerful, with 360, 400 and 440 cc engine sizes being tried. Karsmakers, however, was dogged with injury problems – specifically a broken leg and cartilage trouble – but by the end of the year he had amassed 45 points, including second place in the Canadian GP – to give him tenth place overall.

That year Smith cleaned up in the 125 cc National Championship again and collected a sensational double victory in the US 125 cc round of this new world championship series.

Smith's successes prompted Honda to send him over to Europe to contest most 125 cc grands prix in 1976, while Karsmakers returned to the 500 cc fray. Both men were given faster bikes – the emphasis on Honda Japan's machine development having switched away from the 250 cc class to 125 and 500 cc machinery.

That year Karsmakers gave Honda their first ever 500 cc grand prix success when he won the final leg of the Italian GP. But again he was dogged by injury problems, and the end of the year saw him again in tenth place with 50 points.

Smith enlivened the European scene on his first visit with some spirited riding – he repeated his double US GP victory of 1975 and won races in Denmark and Italy. By the end of the year

SCOTT
HONDA
HONDA
7

Honda's first attempt at an open class machine. This one displaces 450 cc and it's being campaigned by Pierre Karsmakers

he had settled in fourth place. A terrific achievement.

Karsmakers quit at the end of 1976 after failing to achieve a long-term development contract with Honda, and for 1977 Honda America signed 'Bad' Brad Lackey – 1972 National Champion on CZ and Kawasaki – and a man already well established in Europe on Husqvarna machinery.

Lackey – fifth in the world in 1976 – teamed up with Jim Pomeroy, who was to contest US national 500 cc events only. Tommy Croft who had scored a few points in the US 500 cc GP the previous year stayed with Honda's Team Red for 1977.

Lackey's first year was a good one: he scored several wins and finished the year in fourth place ... his own personal best-ever result. Rounding off 1977 Pomeroy won one leg of the US 500 cc grand prix and Honda rider Warren Reid pulled off a win and a third place in the Canadian 125 cc GP. But the most important decision in Honda's bid for moto cross domination came mid-way through 1977 in London, England.

At that time go-ahead Honda UK Senior Manager Gerald Davison was pressing hard for his company to get involved in the European racing scene. He was keen on the endurance road racing championship, but saw in moto cross a real prospect of success. 'We had the obvious contender in reigning British Champion Graham Noyce' he recalls. 'It was just a matter of convincing Japan that this was the way to go.'

Never one to give up easily Davison kept up the pressure on Japan and within a remarkably short period they said *Yes*. Davison entered into secret negotiations with Noyce whose contract with the West German Maico firm had until the end of the year to run.

Secret negotiations they may have been but you cannot keep these things quiet for long. By the end of the grands prix season in September the rumour that Noyce was to sign for Honda exploded onto the front pages of the British weekly press.

Officially Honda and Noyce denied the reports, but by December the secret was out. Official confirmation had to wait until January 1978, however, when a dozen pressmen were invited to Honda UK's Chiswick, West London headquarters to witness Noyce sign a contract to race for Honda in the 1978 world championships.

This contract was certainly the most lucrative ever signed by a British moto cross rider and made Noyce a very wealthy young man. The agreement was with Honda UK who set up the whole deal, but they in turn had a contract with Japan who funded the effort and supplied the bikes.

Right from the word go Davison decided that the grand prix effort would be small, compact and efficient. The team would consist of Noyce and a top-class mechanic ... that is all. But of course Noyce would have access to the big Honda workshops in Frankfurt, West Germany which would also serve as their European base.

The first priority of Honda UK was to secure the 1978 British championship, but this was not Noyce's. He was after the glittering prize – the world 500 cc championship, as he had first won the British title in 1976 and again easily in 1977 (there really was not anyone else in the same class as him).

A young country boy from Fairoak, Hampshire, Noyce had spent most of his life racing moto cross. Encouraged by his father Tom the young Noyce started racing in schoolboy events when nine years old and eventually secured the British schoolboy moto cross championship. His early racing career began on a Husqvarna-engined British Rickman machine and quickly he began to establish himself. In 1973 he finished sixth in the ill-fated British 125 cc class and the following year contested both 125 and 250 cc classes. He campaigned a Maico in the 125 cc, finishing a creditable second, and took the Rickman to tenth place in the 250 cc championship.

The 1975 season saw the young Noyce – still a teenager – really prove that on skill and ability at least he was more than a match for the British veterans. It seemed it was only on maturity and experience that he fell a little short. In the new open-class British championship he came within an ace of taking the title, but a crash in the final round meant that he finished third behind veterans Vic Allan and Vic Eastwood. The Auto Cycle Union, Britain's governing body of motor cycle sport, recognised his ability and put the young Noyce into the British moto cross team for the *Trophee* and *Moto Cross Des Nations* where he helped his country to third place.

During 1975 Noyce did his level best to get as many rides in the 125 cc grands prix as he could – he badgered organisers, cadged lifts abroad and pestered his way to start lines throughout Europe. Racing his Maico as well as a borrowed Husqvarna his persistence paid off – by the end of the year he had amassed a grand total of 13 points. Enough to place him 17th in the title standings.

In 1976 Noyce annihilated the opposition in the British championship. Armed with the experience gained in the 125 cc races he took on the world's best in the 500 cc class with a factory Maico. A fast learner, Noyce kept on improving: third overall in the opening round in Switzerland, second in Austria and then a grand prix leg win in Britain ... at the end of the year he finished a terrific fourth in the championship behind such greats as De Coster, Gerrit Wolsink, and Adolf Weil.

In contrast 1977 was a disappointing year. He finished only eighth in the 500 cc World Championship but there was still the consolation of his second British title – achieved with consummate ease.

And so we come to 1978 – Noyce's debut year

The man who very nearly brought Honda their first moto cross title in 1978 – American rider Brad Lackey

Graham Noyce signs for Honda at the company's headquarters in Chiswick, West London, in January 1978. On Noyce's left is race chief Gerald Davison, on his right is Kazuo Shimizu, who was managing director at the time

DEBUT
HONDA
TURBO

with Honda. As mentioned earlier Noyce's grand prix team was deliberately kept small and compact, but at the grands prix themselves, although the Lackey and Noyce camps were separate units, advice and help were often exchanged. There were no team orders: both men knew that they would give no quarter nor ask it – their objective was to reach the chequered flag first.

But 1978 was not destined to be Noyce's year – although still improving he seemed to suffer from the same problems that dogged him in 1977. His 'balls-out' riding style introduced a new problem – his Honda kept slipping its chain, costing valuable time.

However, 1978 was Lackey's year – Lackey who for many years had persevered as the only Yank on the grands prix circuits rode his heart out. The only man who could beat him was the Flying Finn Heikki Mikkola on his fast Yamaha.

Lackey won in Austria, tied on points in

Above: *Noyce chases US Honda teamster Marty Smith at sunny Carlsbad Raceway in the 1978 US Grand Prix*

Opposite: *the beautifully-styled and impressive CX500 Turbo*

Brad Lackey gets the big works Honda into a powerslide in 1978

France, was runner-up in Finland and Germany and beat Mikkola in Britain. But at the end of the day Lackey's occasional breakdown and crashes spelled disaster – he failed to finish six grands prix races to Mikkola's one failure and when the points were totalled he trailed new World Champion Mikkola by 85 points in runner-up position.

Noyce scored some creditable results, most memorable of which was his third place overall (including a runner-up place in the second leg) in the Luxembourg GP. But mostly he scored only once in a grand prix and then the scores were poor.

It would be unkind to suggest that Noyce's debut year with Honda had been a failure – far from it, for no one can call seventh place in the world a failure. But he definitely did not come up to expectations and the problem seems to be – in retrospect – a personal crisis in his career. After all, he had been getting better and better at a terrific pace, and now he was levelling off ... it must have been difficult to accept.

The year 1979 proved to be the turning point for Noyce ... and Honda. Here the key was men and their motivation. For 1979 Honda came up with Bill Buchka as Noyce's mechanic: a brilliant spanner-man who became Noyce's confidante and friend. A former racer himself Buchka, an American, was able to curb Noyce's socialising, build up his confidence and remind him that he was capable of winning the title provided that he did not throw caution to the wind.

The factory, through the Belgian importer, had also signed up handsome French-speaking Belgian André Malherbe to replace Brad Lackey who had quit to join Kawasaki. In many ways Malherbe was a protégé of Noyce's – he was of the same age group but backed by his wealthy father had got off to a high speed start by winning the very first 125 cc international championship.

Since that easy win he had switched to race an Austrian KTM with great maturity – in 1977 he finished in third place in the 250 cc championship and in 1978 moved up to the 500 cc class, and had a consistent year to finish sixth ... just ahead of Noyce.

The 1979 season began in the best possible way for Noyce – two second places over the hillside track near Sittendorf in Austria were enough to ensure him of an overall victory. And it's inter-

The dust really flies as Noyce blasts into a bank in the 1978 Danish Grand Prix. Just coming into the picture is Brad Lackey

esting to look at that result because it illustrates Noyce's increasing maturity and the approach that ensured his world championship.

In neither race did Noyce make a do-or-die effort to pass the race leader – a sifficult thing to do at Sittendorf. Rather he bided his time, keeping risks to a minimum. First-race victor Belgian Ivan Van Den Broeck was easily the fastest man but Noyce knew that he was an unlikely contender for the title so opted out of a battle with him. In the second race former team-mate Brad Lackey finally took the lead from Noyce after a close-quarters dice.

Guided by Buchka, Noyce progressed through the series racing intelligently, accumulating points in every round while Lackey – in particular – and Malherbe fared somewhat more erratically.

In France he collected a second behind local hero Jean-Jacques Bruno and a seventh place; another second place, behind Lackey followed in Sweden. But whereas Lackey retired in race two Noyce went on to sixth place and more world championship points.

The Italian Grand Prix followed and here Noyce racked up two third places, riding superbly in the heat of Gallarate while the winning was done by a very much on-form Heikki Mikkola who was bringing to an end an incredible career.

Now as the grand prix scene shifted to the West Coast of America – the Southern California moto cross track at Carlsbad – Noyce was leading the Dutch Suzuki veteran Gerrit Wolsink by 77 points to 56. Carlsbad was a problem for Noyce. He knew that Wolsink had been a regular winner over this bone-hard permanent track. He also knew that Lackey would be desperate to win the USGP (a race he had never won) and show his Kawasaki bosses that he was worth the big time contract he had signed.

It would be an exaggeration to say that Noyce was brilliant at Carlsbad, but he rode with great maturity to finish runner-up to Wolsink whose win plus a third place showed that, at Carlsbad, he was still the king. But the gruelling pace and burning heat of the Californian sun in mid-June chopped the field down dramatically – only six riders completed both races and one of them was Noyce. Lackey crashed out of race one but scored

A flying Graham Noyce in action the year he won the world 500 cc title – 1979

a creditable victory over Mikkola in race two.

Wolsink's Carlsbad victory carried him over to an overall first place at the next round in Canada – the halfway stage of the championship. But here Noyce really showed his skill: a super start and a cracking pace put him way out in front in the first race ahead of Wolsink and, next time out, third place behind Wolsink and Lackey gave him runner-up spot overall. Malherbe scored mid-way down the field in Canada after dropping out of both races in the USA. Now, with six grands prix gone and six more to go Noyce led the world on 118 points from Wolsink with 108 and Lackey close behind on 104.

From North America the grands prix switched back to Europe and West Germany for the seventh round of the series.

The German Grand Prix was a surprising one: Bruno swept to a first race lead followed by the world champion of a decade earlier, Swede Bengt Aberg, making a surprise comeback on a Maico. Noyce was not on form and finished a lowly sixth. The second race saw Malherbe take the chequered flag from Noyce, the clearest proof that Honda operated no team orders in their squad.

Pressure on Noyce as the scene switched to Great Britain and the Farleigh Castle course was immense. Although he had a previous race win at a British Grand Prix he had yet to take the overall result and really prove himself.

Lackey and Noyce seemed evenly matched in race one but at the chequered flag the American had the advantage. But in race two it was Noyce all the way and the crowd shouted and cheered him on to a fairytale victory and the overall result that he so dearly wanted.

Now 27 points clear of Wolsink, whose best result at Farleigh Castle was a fourth, Noyce's chances of a world title looked excellent, although he dared not think about it too much.

The Swiss Grand Prix came and went with Noyce following Mikkola home in race one and securing fifth next time out. Wolsink, however, was out of luck – he crashed out of race one and could only manage sixth in race two.

As the grand prix scene moved to Holland the pressure switched to Wolsink who desperately needed a win to stave off his imminent dropping from the works Suzuki team. A win on home ground could be just the fillip the big Dutchman needed.

The two battled with each other in both races: the first race was Noyce's with Wolsink runner-up and positions were reversed next time out. A tie on points resulted and the calculations showed that in the championship stakes Noyce now had 207 points to Wolsink's 167 – a 40 points lead.

The battle now shifted to the infamous Belgian hill-top citadel circuit at Namur, where the pundits calculated that with just one round remaining all Noyce had to do was grab 21 points – a second and a third place would do – and he would be the new champion.

Noyce knew that this was no time for heroics – ride an intelligent race and keep going ... that was his plan. In the event it was all decided in the first race: Noyce took second place on the first lap behind old stager Roger De Coster (Suzuki), and whilst holding third behind André Malherbe his pit signals told him not to try any hell for leather runs – Wolsink had crashed out of the race. That meant his only challenger for the 1979 title had gone – he could afford to finish fifth and still become the champion.

In the final analysis he finished third officially (actually fourth behind Belgian 125 cc GP rider Harry Everts who was not eligible for the official results) and became the first British world moto cross champion for 14 years. Of course Noyce was elated: 'I'm over the moon – this is what I've worked for,' he said afterwards at a Honda champagne reception at the trackside.

The final grand prix in Luxembourg was an undistinguished one for Noyce – he scored only a fourth place, first time out and crashed out of race two. But the final reckoning – the result that really *mattered* – meant that Graham Noyce was the 1979 world 500 cc moto cross champion for Honda with a hefty 225 points tally. And just for the record, Wolsink came home runner-up on 177 points with Malherbe, riding in his debut year with Honda, in third place with 176 points.

The history books, then, show that Honda came onto the grand prix moto cross scene in 1975 – with a definite lack of ballyhoo – and walked off with the glittering prize in the form of the 500 cc world championship just four years later. Not bad – Mr Miyakoshi must have been pleased!

Honda swept on to more success in 1980, but a series of mishaps and crashes, culminating in a serious accident in Italy, ruled Noyce out of sharing in that success. Instead, it fell to Malherbe, riding a masterly championship series with a skill belying his relative lack of experience in the 500 cc class, to clinch the title for Honda for a second year in succession.

The record shows that Malherbe's title came with nine victories, three of them doubles, a fantastic achievement that made him 1980 world champion with 235 points – 14 more than closest rival Brad Lackey.

Honda, though, were to be even more successful in 1981. As many pundits had predicted, Malherbe again swept all before him to take his second title in a row, but this time he was chased hard by a recently recovered Noyce. At the season's end Honda had first and second places – Malherbe and Noyce – and their tally card showed three world 500 cc titles in a row.

But what really stood the world of moto cross on its head was the extraordinary happenings in the two team moto cross events that traditionally close the season in early September.

In 1981 Honda America had signed the legendary Belgian multi-world champion Roger

Graham Noyce on the last lap of the second heat in the 1983 500 cc Austrian GP, riding to victory in front of Hakan Carlqvist of Sweden on a Yamaha

De Coster to mastermind their team entries in the 250 cc *Trophée Des Nations* and 500 cc *Moto Cross Des Nations* events. De Coster persuaded the US officials that an all-Honda team was most likely to succeed . . . and he was proved to be more right than even he surely imagined.

Under De Coster's expert, experienced guidance, the American team swept all before them to clinch first the *Trophée* in Capel Lommel, Belgium and finally the *Moto Cross* over in Bielstein, West Germany. The team consisted of professional works Honda riders: Danny La Porte, Johnny O'Mara, Chuck Sun and Donnie Hansen. De Coster made sure his men were riding works Hondas best suited to the sandy going he knew so well – 'Stadium' bikes fitted with jumbo petrol tanks, so they could be ridden balls-out in the fuel-sapping conditions. As the event is a team one, team placings matter far more than individual results, so despite the fact that a Belgian – André Vromans (Yamaha) – won both races in Belgium, it was the American's tally of 20 points accumulated through second, third and fourth places in race one and second, third and sixth in race two that carried the day. The achievement was America's first international moto cross team-victory and proof, if any were needed, of Honda's moto cross superiority.

The *Moto Cross Des Nations* – an event incidentally carrying world championship status – was a similar Honda America benefit. The same team went – this time on 480 cc machines – and although a race victory eluded them, team riding tactics masterminded by De Coster carried the day.

The US team's relatively high total of 42 points reflects their slightly disappointing individual results, but the fact that they won illustrates their superiority as a team. For the Americans' superbly-prepared machines lasted the distance and they managed to pack more men and machines into the top finishers than anyone else.

Bad luck struck the seemingly unstoppable Malherbe-Honda partnership in 1982, however. Malherbe started the season well with a double victory on the big new monoshock Honda, but halfway through the series, while just five points adrift of Brad Lackey, now on a Suzuki, he was badly injured in a crash that caused him to miss the remaining five grands prix. So Honda's three-year reign at the top of 500 cc world moto cross had come to an end. But all was not lost for Roger De Coster and his American team came to the rescue.

Once again De Coster had signed up for the USA an all-Honda team for the international team moto cross events, and once again they triumphed. The 1982 team of Danny Chandler, Johnny O'Mara, Jim Gibson and David Bailey literally came, saw and conquered. And this time race victory was theirs as European newcomer Danny Chandler took a double victory at the

André Malherbe leads Roger De Coster (now Honda Moto Cross team manager) in the Belgian 500 cc Grand Prix of 1980

Britain's latest grand prix challenger Dave Thorpe on the latest water-cooled 480 cc machine with Pro Link rear suspension

West German track at Gaildorf, near Stuttgart, where the 250 cc *Trophée Des Nations* was contested. The American's total of 23 points was fully 11 better than runner's-up Belgium, and they were the only team to pack four men into the top ten in both races.

On to Wohlen, Switzerland for the *Moto Cross Des Nations* where the American Honda team again triumphed, this time shattering the opposition as Chandler took another double victory and the team finished on 24 points humbling the Belgians by 16 points.

So Honda may have finished 1982 without an individual moto cross title, but the Americans ended up as the world champions of moto cross. An acceptable consolation prize for Honda.

For the 1983 season Honda strengthened their moto cross squad by signing the brilliant young English rider Dave Thorpe to team with their former World Champions Graham Noyce and André Malherbe. And, determined to win back the 500 cc crown from Suzuki, the three factory riders were equipped with brand new bikes. These feature water-cooling (previously only used on the smaller engines) which have allowed the technicians to push the horse power up to the 60 mark without overheating.

Proving the strength of the 1983 Honda challenge, Noyce and Malherbe opened the season with a win and a second place apiece at the 500 cc Swiss Moto Cross Grand Prix and they went on to dominate the next two rounds of the series, in Austria and West Germany. This meant that after three rounds (with two races at each) Malherbe led the World Championship with three outright wins from Noyce with two wins. Thorpe started the season well too with places in Switzerland and West Germany as well as challenging for the British Championship.

Trials

Despite the fact that Honda have never made great efforts in the trials world, concentrating on road racing and moto cross, they have supported selected riders with success. Above, left: England's Rob Shepherd, who won the 1977 British Trials Championship. Above: Japan's leading trials rider Kiyoteru Hattori in action during the 1980 Scottish Six Days Trial. Left: Belgian Eddy Lejeune who won the 1982 World Championship guns his Honda over a hazard during the French round of the series. Opposite: Lejeune again – this time tackling a spectacular rocky stream in France

Castrol
Gecel
4
CHAMPIONNAT DU MONDE
LES ROUSSES
HONDA

Road Test Digest

This chapter attempts to highlight the outstanding Honda roadster machines with the help of the extensive archives of 'Motor Cycle Weekly'. By using extracts from the contemporary road tests, the good – and bad – points of the road-going Hondas are revealed.

The model that really put Honda on the map in Europe and broke down the sales resistance to 'Made in Japan' motor cycles was the 250 cc Dream Super Sport – the factory's first European-style machine and now a classic sought by enthusiasts around the world.

Reports of the growth of the Japanese motor cycle industry and of Honda in particular appeared in the British two-wheeler press of the 1950s from time to time – but until Honda's appearance in the 1959 Isle of Man TT races no one had taken the oriental threat seriously. That may seem strange in the 1980s but those were very different days. For a start the war was not long finished and atrocities committed by the Japanese against allied servicemen were still fresh in the minds of the buying public. Secondly the Japanese still had to prove the quality of their products. The majority of goods originating from the East in the early post-war years were poor copies of European or American originals, badly made and unreliable.

Thirdly, the British motor cycle industry, although on the decline, was still a powerful force and it did not take kindly to British motor cycle publications – and British dealers – giving space to publicise rival machines from Japan. In fact in those early days many dealers were given the stark choice: them or us. And the magazines of the day were threatened with the loss of advertising revenue if road tests of the new machines were printed.

The first short test to appear in *The Motor Cycle* was published on 30 June 1960. Road tester David Dixon had borrowed a 250 cc Dream while in the Isle of Man to cover the TT races. This was the early oriental-style machine with leading link forks and rectangular rear suspension units. At that time no Honda machines had been sold to the British public and Maico (Great Britain) Ltd were negotiating to import three models for the UK market. Dixon's impressions did little to excite the sporting motor cyclist ... 'the Dream is a gentleman's motor cycle, as docile a twin as ever purred over the Mountain lap, a model designed to provide true armchair motor cycling.'

Even in those now far away days the specification included an electric starter and built-in trafficators, but the tester was forced to admit that: 'the Dream's performance is average by contemporary standards' while the ... 'roadholding, suspension and braking are more than adequate for the Dream's performance.' In other words it was a bit of a slug that was likely to appeal to the commuter market because of its refinements, but was no threat to the more lucrative sports machine sector. Price had been fixed at £238 and imports did in fact start later that year along with the excellent little 125 cc Benly twin.

This model was the first to be given the full road test treatment by *The Motor Cycle* with electronically-timed speed figures. The write-up published in May 1961 starts with a blast: 'Any lingering notion that Japanese machines are shoddy imitations of West European designs should have been buried several years ago. If it has not, the Honda Benly gives the answer. The bold and intriguing concept of a 125 cc overhead-camshaft roadster twin peaking at 9,500 rpm makes a mockery of a charge of imitation. At the same time the Benly's finish and excellent engineering are not only far from shoddy but comparable with the world's best.'

That's straight talking and one suspects it was aimed at the British manufacturers of the day who continued to produce lightweights based on pre-war designs. Following up hard the test continued ... 'But the Benly's trump card is its sheer value for money. For less than £180, including purchase tax, it offers a luxury specification including push-button starting, transmission enclosure and flashing turn indicators, while its above-average road performance goes hand in hand with quietness, cleanliness, economy and tirelessness.'

For the record the little Benly had a cruising speed of 50-55 mph (80-88 kph), never averaged less than 85 mpg (3.32 litres/100 km) and recorded a highest one-way speed during the timed test session of 66 mph (106 kph) with a two-way top

The first Hondas imported into Europe had lumpy oriental styling. This is the 125 cc C92 twin of 1960

speed average of 63 mph (101 kph).

The Benly, although less oriental in appearance than the 1960 Dream, retained some of the old Honda styling with square headlamp, cumbersome-looking pressed-steel leading-link front fork and deep mudguarding front and rear – but all that was changed on the 250 cc Dream Super Sport introduced later in 1961 and tested by *The Motor Cycle* in December that year. This was a machine aimed squarely at the European-American market – a lightweight sports machine with elegant good looks, an impressive specification and performance to match – all at a bargain price.

Underlining the part that racing successes had played in getting Honda's sale message over the test started thus: 'Over the past two years, the name Honda has cropped up with the regularity of a jack-in-the-box. Such is the magnitude of the firm's racing successes that "Honda" has achieved a place in the British lay-public vocabulary. But have racing successes any bearing on production quality? Does racing really improve the breed? That the answer to both these questions is a decided "yes" is immediately obvious.'

The test continued: 'The Dream Super Sport is

Benly Twin

Specification

Engine: 125 cc (44×41 mm) overhead camshaft parallel twin. Two ball main bearings; caged roller big-end bearings. Wet sump lubrication, 2 pt (1.14 litres) capacity. Compression ratio, 8.3 to 1. One Keihin PW18H carburettor.
Transmission: Primary helical gears. Wet, multiplate clutch and four-speed gearbox. Chain final drive. Overall ratios: 26.66, 16.42, 12.13 and 8.97 to 1.
Electrical Equipment: Coil ignition with auto-advance. 6-volt, 50-watt alternator, charging 11-amp-hour battery. 4.5-in diameter headlamp with 35/25-watt main bulb.
Brakes: Both approximately 6.5-in diameter; finger adjusters.
Suspension: Leading-link front and pivoted rear forks, both controlled by coil-spring-and-hydraulic units.
Dimensions: Wheelbase, 49 in (124.5 cm); ground clearance, 5 in (12.7 cm).
Kerb Weight: 266 lb (121 kg) with 0.5 gallon of fuel.
Fuel Capacity: 1.9 gallons (8.63 litres).

Performance

Best One-way Speed: 66 mph (106 kph); wet track, moderate three-quarter wind.
Best Standing Quarter-mile: 22.8 sec/55 mph (88.5 kph).
Fuel Consumption: 109 mpg at 30 mph; 98 mpg at 40 mph; 89 mpg at 50 mph.
Braking Distance: From 30 mph, 30 ft 6 in.

The superbly styled 250 cc CB72 Honda of 1962 did much to break down sales resistance to Japanese machines

CB72 Dream Super Sport

Specification

Engine: 274 cc (54 × 54 mm) overhead camshaft parallel twin. Two ball and two roller main bearings; roller big-end bearings. Wet sump lubrication, 2.75 pt (1.6 litres) capacity. Compression ratio, 9.5 to 1. Two Keihin carburettors.
Transmission: Chain primary drive. Wet, multiplate clutch and four-speed gearbox. Chain final drive. Overall ratios: 18.63, 11.1, 7.83 and 6.68 to 1.
Electrical Equipment: Coil ignition with auto-advance. 12-volt, 60-watt alternator, charging 9-amp-hour battery. Electric starter motor. 6-in diameter headlamp with 35/25-watt main bulb.
Brakes: Both approximately 8-in diameter, twin-leading shoe rear; finger adjusters.
Suspension: Telescopic front fork with hydraulic damping. Pivoted rear fork controlled by spring-and-hydraulic units with three-position adjustment for load.
Dimensions: Wheelbase, 51 in (129.5 cm); ground clearance, 6 in (15.2 cm).
Kerb Weight: 336 lb (152 kg) with 2 pt of fuel.
Fuel Capacity: 2.5 gallons (11.3 litres).

Performance

Best One-way Speed: 91 mph (144.8 kph); slight three-quarter wind
Best Standing Quarter-mile: 18.1 sec/75 mph (120.7 kph).
Fuel Consumption: 106 mpg at 30 mph; 90 mpg at 40 mph; 67 mpg at 50 mph; 64 mpg at 60 mph.
Braking Distance: From 30 mph, 35 ft.

far and away the fastest production two-fifty yet tested by *The Motor Cycle* and, but for slight overgearing, it could well be faster.' Highest one way speed during the test was 91 mph (146 kph) with an average of 89 mph for the 'there and back' runs. Top speed in third (surprisingly the gearbox was only a four-speeder) was an impressive 86 mph which emphasised the fact that top was very much an overdrive type of gear.

Talking about performance the test stated: ... 'the Dream Super Sport would hold 70-75 mph (112-120 kph) for the entire length of the M1 motorway with the rider normally seated. Undulating main roads called for frequent use of third if 70-plus was to be maintained.' Pretty impressive for a two-fifty even now and sensational for 1961, even though the newly opened M1 was in those days only some 60 miles (96.5 km) long. The test concluded: 'That a machine of such full blooded performance should at the same time be so unobtrusive and docile reflects tremendous credit on a firm founded only 13 years ago.'

A 305 cc version (the CB77) followed and during the test gave a best one-way speed of 95 mph (153 kph). Again the tester was impressed: 'There is no mystery about the growing popularity of the 305 cc Super Sport Honda. Its performance would do credit to a five-hundred

An enlarged version of the CB72, the CB77 was powered by a 305 cc twin-cylinder engine. This shows the machine as sold in 1964

and the standard specification includes items that are usually extras or, even, luxuries. Moreover the price is distinctly competitive.'

The 305 cc model, at that time the biggest Honda offered for sale, was virtually the two-fifty bored out from 54 to 60 mm to give bore and stroke dimensions of 60 × 54 mm. Like the smaller engine the cranks were set at 180 degrees to one another unlike the traditional British vertical twins in which the pistons rose and fell together.

By this time Maico (Great Britain) Ltd, had been replaced as the concessionaires for the UK by European Honda Motor Trading and the sales drive was really underway. An updated version of the Benly, the 125 cc CB92 was tested in November 1963 and recorded an improved top speed of 69 mph (111 kph) with a one-way run at 73 mph (117 kph). The little step-through C50 was introduced and the more powerful 90 cc version added in 1965 – and slightly improved are still selling well to commuters many years later!

However, for the motor cyclist the next big step by Honda was the introduction of their first true mid-range machine – the CB450 with 445 cc vertical twin engine. This went on sale early in 1966 and recorded 100 mph (160 kph) on the timing strip at MIRA with the rider in a racing

CB77 Super Sport

Specification

Engine: 305 cc (60 × 54 mm) overhead camshaft parallel twin. Two ball and two roller main bearings; roller big-end bearings. Wet sump lubrication, 3.5 pt (2 litres) capacity. Compression ratio, 9.5 to 1. Two Keihin carburettors.
Transmission: Chain primary drive. Wet, multiplate clutch and four-speed gearbox. Chain final drive. Overall ratios: 17.48, 10.42, 7.33 and 6.27 to 1.
Electrical Equipment: Coil ignition with auto-advance. 12-volt, 160-watt alternator, charging 9-amp-hour battery. Starter motor. 6-in diameter headlamp with 35/25-watt main bulb.
Brakes: Both 7.875-in diameter, twin leading shoes; finger adjusters.
Suspension: Telescopic front fork with hydraulic damping. Pivoted rear fork controlled by spring-and-hydraulic units with three-position adjustment for load.
Dimensions: Wheelbase, 51 in (129.5 cm); ground clearance, 5.5 in (14 cm).
Kerb Weight: 360 lb (163 kg) with one gallon of fuel.
Fuel Capacity: 2.25 gallons (10.2 litres).

Performance

Best One-way Speed: 95 mph (153 kph); strong side wind.
Best Standing Quarter-mile: 16.8 sec/76 mph (122 kph).
Fuel Consumption: 96 mpg at 30 mph; 88 mpg at 40 mph; 66 mpg at 50 mph; 60 mpg at 60 mph.
Braking Distance: From 30 mph, 31 ft.

crouch and 93.5 mph (150 kph) sitting up. Basically the CB450 was similar to the earlier twins although the cylinders were set upright instead of being inclined forward. Bore and stroke were well oversquare at 70 × 57.8 mm and the engine had double overhead camshafts instead of the single camshaft of the earlier twins. The original model, affectionately known as the Black Bomber because of the standard black and chrome finish, was replaced in 1969 by an improved model with five-speed gearbox and the power upped from 43 to 45 bhp at 9,000 rpm.

The previous year Honda had replaced the much loved CB250 Super Sport with another model with the same designation but very different looks. Gone was the fine blend of oriental and European styling – in its place was a rather dumpy westernised machine. Very cobby and business-like but lacking the elegant good looks of its predecessor. Said the *Motor Cycle* test of March 1968: 'Honda's new two-fifty, the single overhead camshaft CB250 Super Sport, is more than the first five-speeder the factory has put on the British market. It is also the forerunner of the latest in big-bike Honda styling.'

Bore and stroke of the new engine were 56 × 50.6 mm and as usual with Honda twins the cranks were set at 180 degrees. A 175 cc model with the old styling was retained for a while, and with a top speed of some 80 mph (128 kph) and a

Above: *Dutch tester Gerhard Klomps astride a CB250SS during a 1968 road test*

Opposite, top: *road tester Peter Fraser swings the CB450 around a bend during a 1966 road test*

Opposite, bottom: *the CB250SS of 1968*

CB750

Specification

Engine: 736 cc (61 × 63 mm) single-overhead camshaft, transverse, in-line four. Five plain main bearings; plain big-end bearings. Dry sump lubrication, 6 pt (3.4 litres) capacity. Compression ratio, 9 to 4. Four 28-mm choke Keihin carburettors; paper element air filter. Claimed maximum power, 67 bhp at 8,000 rpm.
Transmission: Duplex primary chain. Wet, multiplate clutch and five-speed gearbox. Secondary by gears from gearbox output shaft to countershaft. Chain final drive. Overall ratios: 14.01, 9.57, 7.47, 6.25 and 5.26 to 1.
Electrical Equipment: Coil ignition. 12-volt, 210-watt alternator, charging 14-amp-hour battery. 6.6-in diameter headlamp with 50/40-watt main bulb. Starter motor.
Brakes: Hydraulically-operated 11.7-in diameter disc front; 7-in diameter single-leading shoe rear.
Suspension: Telescopic front fork with two-way hydraulic damping; pivoted rear fork controlled by hydraulic struts with three-position adjustments for load.
Dimensions: Wheelbase, 57.5 in (146 cm); ground clearance, 6.5 in (16.5 cm).
Kerb Weight: 481 lb (218 kg) with full fuel tank.
Fuel Capacity: 5 gallons (22.7 litres) including reserve.

Performance

Best One-way Speed: 118 mph (189.9 kph); still air, drizzle, damp track.
Best Standing Quarter-mile: 13.6 sec/101 mph (162.5 kph).
Fuel Consumption: Approximately 45 mpg overall.

Honda's first superbike – the four-cylinder CB750 of 1969

selling price around £190 – £80 less than the two-fifty – it was a firm favourite and earned the praise of *Motor Cycle*: 'For a combination of performance and refinement, with plenty of change left out of £200, the CD175 takes some beating. In spite of its 80-plus top speed and 10,500 rpm, it is quiet and comfortable to ride and gives more than 100 mpg (2.82 litres/100 km) at 40 mph (64 kph).

About this time rumours began to circulate that Honda were busy designing and developing a machine to challenge the hard pressed British industry for the only corner of the market in which it still had machines that sold well – the big-bike over 500 cc category. In fact a race was on between Honda and BSA-Triumph to introduce their new superbikes – both 750 cc models.

Honda were the first to get their machine, the CB750, into full production and it went on to be the most successful big motor cycle of all time – a million being sold all over the world within the next decade. To gauge the impact of the machine one has to realise that it was the first Japanese machine of over 500 cc to be marketed; it was the first mass produced four-cylinder motor cycle to go on sale and it was available in the UK less than ten years after a handful of dealers began to sell the first lightweight oriental-style Hondas in Europe.

Motor Cycle tested the CB750 in July 1969 and it is worth quoting at length from chief road tester David Dixon's article. 'So much speculation has preceded the arrival of the Honda CB750 that anticipation could have outstripped realisation. It hasn't. After tests in Germany I would say that, assuming production models match the demonstration job I rode, the bikes will more than live up to what we expect.

'How much the fantastic racing successes of the Hondas have influenced the design is impossible to say but, like all racing fours, 125, 250, 350 and 500 cc, the CB750 has the in-line engine set across the frame. Unlike the racer, though, there is a single overhead camshaft and two valves per cylinder. Also, unlike Mike Hailwood's famous Senior-category bike, the roadster has a full duplex frame, not the backbone type.

'Let's go from the beginning. A tiny electric-starter button by the twistgrip growls the 67 horses into life. A downward dab with the left foot selects bottom gear noiselessly. The experience starts. Any sense of heaviness and bulk which you may have when sitting astride the model for the first time is forgotten within the first few yards. The bike is beautifully balanced.

'The fuel tank, on the knee-grip line, is no wider than that of the average five-hundred. Footrest width match knee width; the reach to the handlebar gives a relaxed position and you feel, immediately, part of the machine. Only a glance down reveals the two outside cylinders projecting into the airstream and confirms the 21.5-inch (54.6-cm) width across the crankcase.

'That the CB750 is not just a rorty man-eater is apparent within the first quarter-mile. Docile and tractable, the engine purrs happily at 3,000 rpm in top gear; that is about 45 mph (72 kph). Tweek the grip and the pick-up is unhesitant; it is so deceptively smooth that you are forgiven for thinking it almost sluggish until the speedometer and wind pressure tell the truth.

'A combination of complete smoothness and effortless torque waft you up to the nineties so rapidly that only the alarming speed at which you rush up to the corners dispels the illusion. The characteristics are quite different from those of super-sports twins of the same capacity. The feeling of violent acceleration of the twins is absent though the rate of acceleration of the four is even swifter. Moreover, the four is still galloping upward after the twins have run out of breath. For instance, at 105 mph (169 kph) the Honda is still accelerating with the rider sitting bolt upright, whereas most other big roadsters I have ridden responded above this speed only when I tucked in as much as possible.

'Gear ratios are well chosen, with the biggest gap – representing 2,600 rpm – between first and second. The spacing between the other ratios represents 1,850, 1,300 and 1,100 rpm respectively.

'On a standing-start quarter-mile test, a good six-fifty twin would probably lead for the initial 100 yards (91 metres). But then the CB750 would overcome its higher weight (around 60 lb/27 kg) and, as the extra horses got into full gallop, the twin would be overhauled. The terminal speed of 101 mph (162.5 kph) at the end of the quarter-mile is among the highest recorded by *Motor Cycle*.

'To achieve this, I found it best to drop the clutch lever around 7,000 rpm and spin off. The longest unbroken black mark stretched for about 15 ft (457 cm) before the rear tyre bit. After six runs of this treatment, the clutch needed a five-minute cooling off period before the slack in the cable returned to normal. Otherwise the clutch was above criticism.

'With the full 14.2-mile (22.85-km) Nürburgring grand-prix circuit at my disposal, I did not spend too much time exploring the docile half of the bike's character. The lure of the famous lap beckoned and it was here that the Honda bared its racing background. Screwing the twistgrip until the revs soared to the 8,500 limit in each gear, I enjoyed some of the most exhilarating miles I have ever known.

'The Nürburgring might have been designed by a demented snake charmer. It has a bewildering assortment of corners and the intervening straights have switchbacks with blind crests, over the final brow of which the road may switch right or left. One of the fastest sections is downhill with flat-out, right-left-right-left swoops between pine trees. Add a sprinkling of rain in places, and occasional damp patches beneath the trees, and you have a circuit as demanding as the Isle of Man Mountain lap.

Honda sprang a surprise when they launched the CB500 four at Daytona in 1972. Here tester John Nutting sets out on a CB500

'Acceleration, roadholding and braking were stressed to the limit. Especially when coming out of medium-fast corners, acceleration was markedly good, with revs soaring to peak extremely rapidly. Because of the twisty track, and the fact that the engine is at its best when buzzing, I found it convenient to stay in fourth – this meant 105 mph (168 kph) on tap by the start of the red sector at 8,500 rpm.

'A worthwhile bonus was to be gained by engaging top at only five places. One of these was on the main straight approaching the start. Tucking in as best I could in a Barbour suit, foiled to some extent by the high-level handle-bar, I let the revs soar into the red at 8,600 before notching top. On a slight depression, the needle moved swiftly to 8,000 rpm – equivalent to 118 mph (190 kph) – before dropping back to a steady 7,800 (116 mph).

'Under dry conditions, when I could have discarded the bulky suit, the lower drag may have given a speed over the 125 mark. With a sports fairing, probably another 10 mph ... Lap time was 12 minutes 4 seconds (equivalent to about 70.6 mph/113.6 kph) and included slowing for a German film crew preparing to blow up a racing car for a crash sequence.

'All this was achieved without any trace of

Opposite, top: *popular single-cylinder lightweight – the CB250RS seen here as catalogued in 1982*

Opposite, bottom: *one of the prettiest bikes of 1982 – the CX500 Euro Sport*

A static shot of the impressive CB500 of 1972

mechanical fuss and with the minimum of exhaust noise. The four separate pipes and reverse-cone megaphone silencers mute the exhaust note and only when the revs soar above 6,000 rpm is the rise in volume audible to the rider. It was not offensive. The only vibration was on approaching peak revs, when a barely perceptible tremor was felt through the right footrest.

'For a machine of its bulk, the Honda handled well. Occasionally I entered corners quicker than I should have done and had to keep the brakes on. Extra effort was then required to lay the model over and this caused some tail-wagging. But normally, cornering was extremely steady, with the model leeching to whatever line I chose. Changing line required some physical effort and resulted in gentle tail wags but this was as much my doing as the machine's.

CB500F

Specification

Engine: 498 cc (56 × 50.6 mm) single-overhead camshaft, transverse, in-line four. Five plain main bearings; plain big-end bearings. Wet sump lubrication, 5.2 pt (2.9 litres) capacity. Compression ratio, 9 to 1. Four 22-mm choke Keihin carburettors; paper element air filter. Claimed maximum power, 50 bhp at 9,000 rpm.
Transmission: Primary by inverted-tooth chain and spur gears through wet multiplate clutch to five-speed gearbox. Chain final drive. Overall ratios: 15.27, 10.6, 8.24, 6.72 and 5.84 to 1.
Electrical Equipment: Twin coil ignition. 12-volt, 200-watt alternator charging 12-amp-hour battery. 7-in diameter headlamp with 35/35-watt main bulb. Starter motor, headlamp flasher.
Brakes: 11-in diameter, hydraulically-operated disc front; 7.5-in diameter drum rear.
Suspension: Hydraulically-damped telescopic front fork; pivoted rear fork controlled by spring-and-hydraulic struts, with three-position adjustment for load.
Dimensions: Wheelbase, 55.5 in (141 cm); ground clearance, 6.5 in (16.5 cm).
Kerb Weight: 450 lb (204 kg) with 2 gallons of fuel.
Fuel Capacity: 3.1 gallons (14.1 litres) including 7 pt reserve.

Performance

Best One-way Speed: 106 mph (170.6 kph); dry track, strong cross wind.
Best Standing Quarter-mile: 15.4 sec/88 mph (141.2 kph).
Fuel Consumption: 72 mpg at 30 mph; 71 mpg at 40 mph; 68 mpg at 50 mph; 64 mpg at 60 mph; 58 mpg at 70 mph.
Braking Distance: From 30 mph, 23 ft 6 in.

'Front and rear suspension are well matched, with rebound damping firm enough to prevent the wallowing and bouncing so often associated with Japanese bikes. On the roughest section of the circuit, a slightly uphill straight tackled at over 100 mph (160 kph), sharp undulations chucked the machine well clear of the road, yet directional stability remained bang on, with scarcely a nod from the steering head.

'The Dunlop's broad profile K81 rear tyre – new from the Japanese factory – provided markedly good adhesion, especially on the treacherously damp patches of the circuit. Under fierce braking both tyres gripped extremely well and far better than any previous Japanese covers with which I have had experience. They were as good as British equivalents.

'The single-disc front brake on the CB750, although not so potent as other disc types I have tried, was smoother than usual with a twin-leading shoe drum brake and the sensitivity of the hydraulic action was reassuring on the dodgy surfaces. The single leading shoe rear brake was undoubtedly powerful; it was light in operation and, under heavy pressure, would squeal the tyre without actually locking. And when repeatedly applied hard from maximum speed, neither brake showed the slightest sign of fading.

'Even allowing for the bias I might have felt by the exhilerating miles I covered on the magnificent Nürburgring circuit, the Honda four ranks as one of the most outstanding machines I have ever ridden. The more I rode it, the more it grew on me. Imports to Britain may not begin for a few months but they will be worth waiting for.'

Pretty impressive . . . and the Honda CB750 was soon a top seller both in America (where it cost less than the rival three-cylinder 750 cc BSA Rocket and Triumph Trident machines) and in Europe. In fact it was so popular that *Motor Cycle* published a second full test nine months later – in April 1970. Highest one-way speed was slightly up at 121 mph (195 kph) with a 115 mph (185 kph) average for runs in opposite directions. The four-cylinder superbike was well and truly launched and since then has been copied by all three rival Japanese motor cycle manufacturers.

To prove the potential of the new machine, and to gain valuable worldwide publicity, Honda produced a small batch of race-kitted models for the 1970 Daytona 200 race in Florida. It was the factory's first racing effort since Mike Hailwood had disputed the world championship grands prix in 1967 and it resulted in a splendid victory for American veteran Dick Mann. Ironically he returned the following year as a member of the rival BSA team and won again but that is another story!

By coincidence Honda launched their next four-cylinder sensation at Daytona in 1972. This was a 500 cc sports tourer but it was not just a smaller version of the incredibly successful CB750. In typical Japanese fashion it was a completely new machine. *Motor Cycle* road tester John Nutting was impressed:

'If you want a yardstick for engine smoothness,

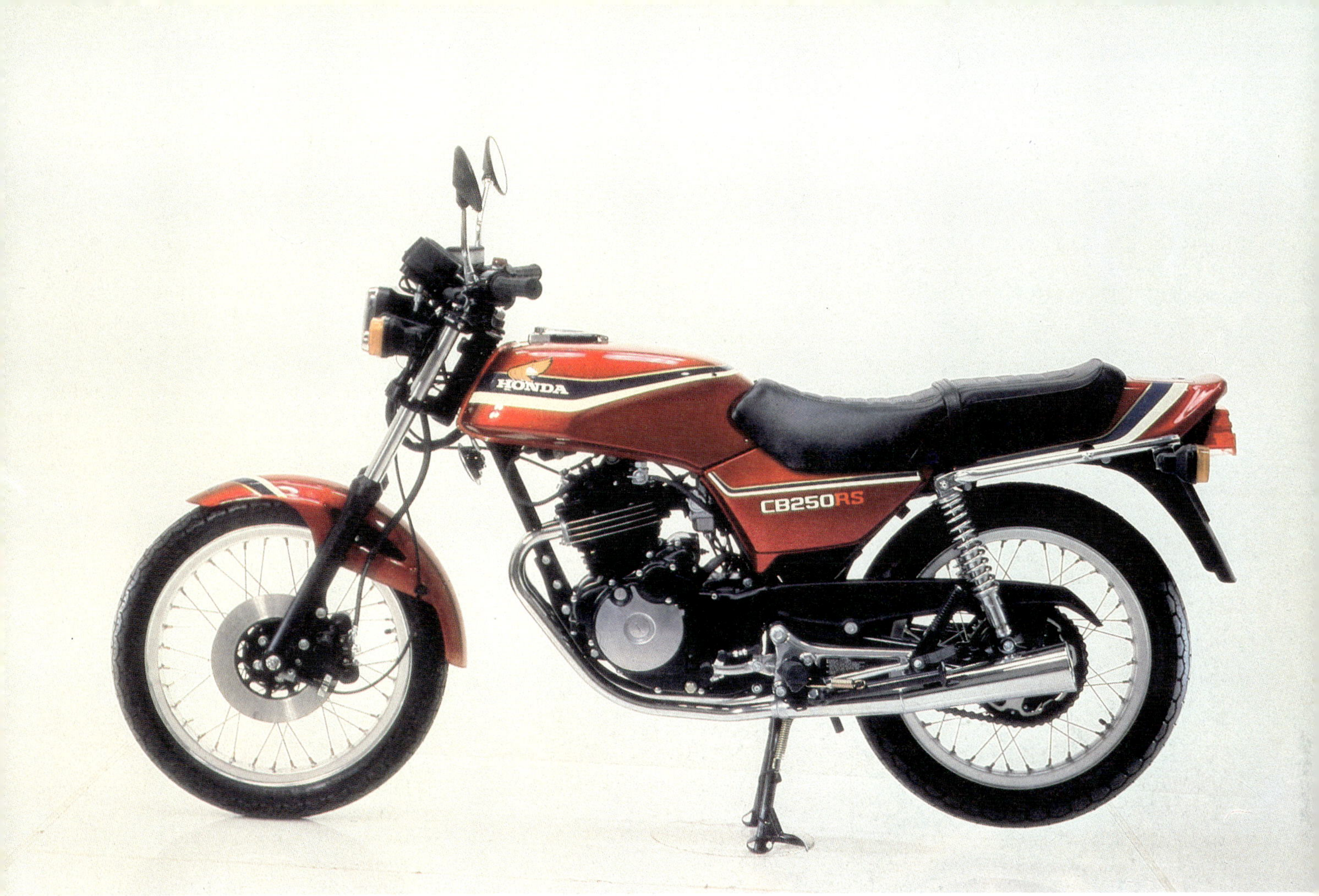
HONDA
CB250RS

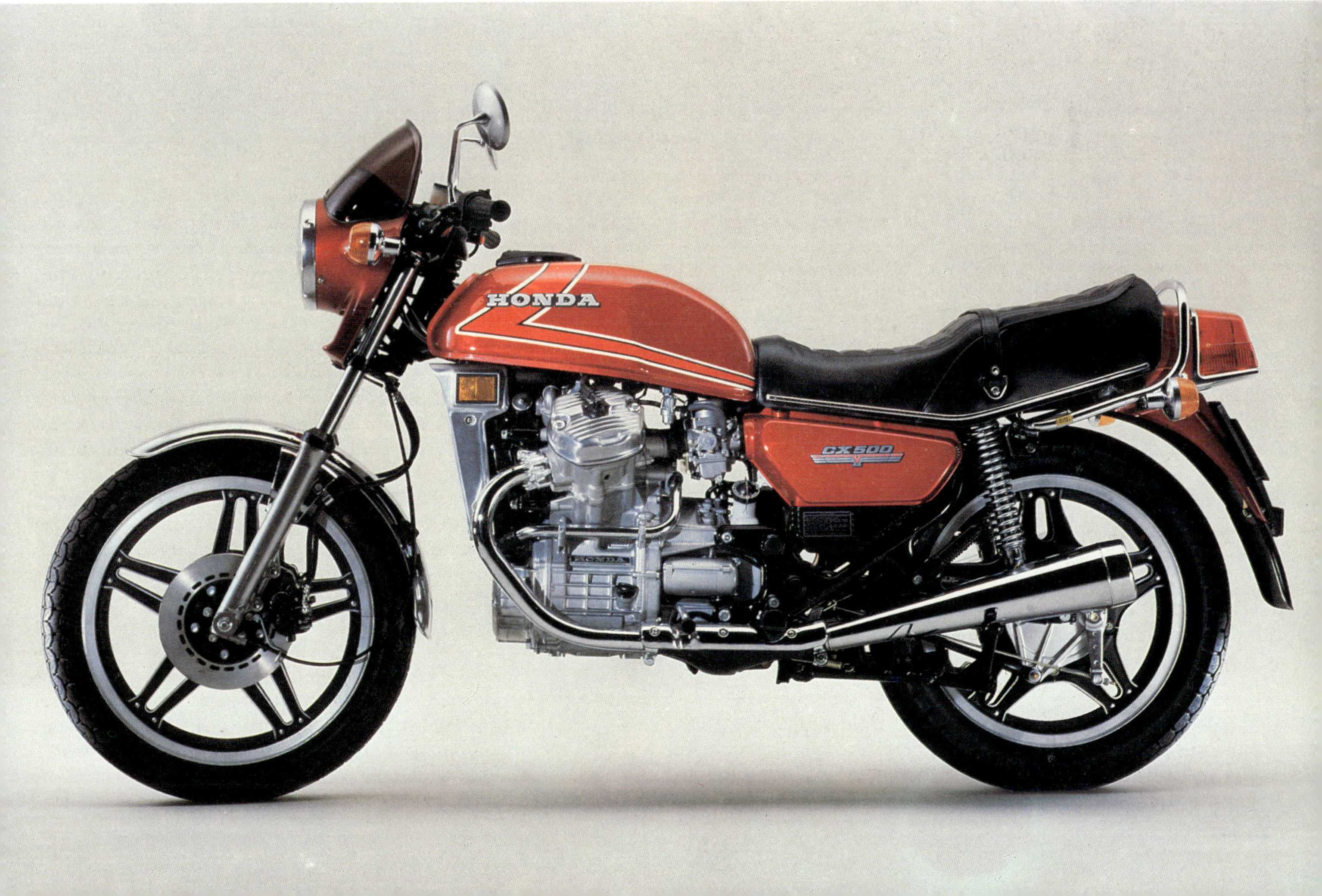
HONDA
CX500

Honda have always paid great attention to ease of maintenance. Here the road tester shows how the battery is attached on the CB500 by a simple elastic strap

the Honda CB500F four is as good a bike as you are likely to find. If the power unit were hidden from view, you could be excused for imagining it was an electric motor. Not only does the latest Honda four in the UK lack the obesity of the CB750 – if anything, it provides even more refinement, too. Straddling the bike you get no great impression of engine width. Indeed, behind the crankcase, the bike is no wider than average. And seat height is a reasonable 31 in (79 cm).

'In appearance the CB500F captures the flavour of the glamorous works racing fours of the 1960s. And although peak power is a claimed 50 bhp at 9,000 rpm, the engine is very tractable at low revs. The machine is just as happy at a walking-pace crawl as at three-figure speeds. It is also uncommonly quiet.

The CB500F has two distinct styles of performance. For sedate travel, you simply keep the revs below 4,000 rpm and the bike glides along like a two-wheeled car. But if you want a really spicy throttle response, you hold the revs above 5,500 by free use of the gearbox. From that engine speed, a tweak of the grip sends the revs rushing up the scale to the 9,200 rpm red mark on the meter.

'At high revs, the pleasant hum of the exhausts could just be heard above the wind roar. And it was only by moving the knees away from the tank that the busy rustle of the valve gear became audible. The most obtrusive mechanical noise was a whine from the primary-drive gears. Though a slight tingle could be felt through the seat at 4,000 rpm, and the images in the right-hand mirror were blurred above 7,000 rpm, the engine was one of the smoothest imaginable. So smooth at top revs, in fact, that a close watch had to be kept on the revmeter during full-throttle acceleration to avoid risk of over-revving.

'At the lower end of the range, the engine was a as docile as a lamb. And rolling the twistgrip right back at traffic halts produced reliable idling at about 1,000 rpm.

'Starting was always easy. The electric motor spun the engine briskly, even when it was cold. For cold starting, the butterfly chokes had to be closed, but it was necessary to open them partially as soon as the engine fired to avoid flooding. In normal conditions, the kickstarter was an ornament. Once the engine was hot, really easy starting could be demonstrated by depressing the pedal by hand!

One of the neatest and most practical Hondas ever built – the SL125 of 1973

'Throughout the 1,100-mile (1,760-km) test, petrol consumption averaged 54 mpg (5.23 litres/ 100 km), and that's good considering plenty of throttle was used whenever possible.

'As soon as it is on the move, the CB500's weight is unnoticed. True the 4.1 inch (10.4 cm) fork trail makes the steering feel dead at low speeds, but little effort was required for slow turns or changes of lock. At high speeds the steering was taut, even on bumpy surfaces, and very stable in bends. Both prop and main stands are well tucked away, and kept clear of the ground during exuberant cornering. The Japanese tyres, though, are a bit below the non-skid standard of British tyres on wet roads.

'The springing was a shade firm and transmitted low-speed bumps to the rider, but prevented any trace of weaving at high speeds.

'The size of the dual seat is ample for pillion riding. A foot wide for the most part, it is slim enough at the front for a rider of average size to stand astride the bike. This advantage is offset by the upholstery, which is shallower than it appears to be and feels hard after several hours of riding. Though the flat handlebar was comfortably positioned, the non-adjustable footrests could with advantage have been set farther back to give the rider a slight forward lean to reduce wind drag on the arms when cruising at high speeds.

'With the engine spinning at only 8,200 rpm at maximum speed, overall gearing is on the high side, and there is no fear of over-revving in top gear. The top three gear ratios are fairly closely spaced, which makes it easy to keep the engine on the boil in high-speed traffic. All gear changes were slick – and so sweet that for upward changes there was no real need to declutch. Neutral was most easily selected before the bike came to rest, otherwise it was awkward to find, and the indicator light in the handlebar panel was not always a reliable guide.

'Some delicacy was needed when feeding in the clutch from a standstill, if the last fraction of lever movement was not to produce a lurch. There was no sign of slip of drag, though the friction discs swelled with heat during our usual series of full-throttle acceleration tests at the MIRA proving ground. They returned to normal when cooled off.

'The performance of the brakes was stupendous. The incredibly short stopping distance, 23 feet 6 inches (7.2 m) from 30 mph (48 kph),

speaks for itself, yet the bike was fully under control when the tests were made. Front-wheel locking was never experienced, though on wet roads the 11 inch disc brake had to be treated with care at low speeds. At high speeds, the action was progressive, though fairly heavy lever pressure was needed. No brake adjustment was required during the test.'

By this time new Hondas were beginning to spew out of the factory at an ever increasing pace as the Japanese factory steadily enlarged their range to fill virtually every gap in the market. One of the first of Honda's dual purpose trail bikes was the neatly styled little SL125 which quickly became a firm favourite with European riders who wanted a machine capable of coping with muddy tracks as well as roads.

After testing an SL125 in 1973 *Motor Cycle* reporter John Ebbrell wrote: 'A rousing little job, it steers nicely, is fast for its size, economical, an easy starter and above all superbly silenced.

'Basically, the SL125 trail bike is the 122 cc single-cylinder, overhead-camshaft, five-speed unit of the CB125S sports roadster built into a new, longer-wheelbase, duplex frame with a 21 inch diameter front wheel and a turned-up exhaust system. Overall gearing is lower than the roadster's, but its all-up weight is some 11 lb (5 kg) more.

'For sheer speed, the SL125 could see off many standard roadsters of the same capacity, let alone trail bikes. It held the red line of 9,500 rpm without difficulty in top gear on the level, two-up – a true speed of 65 mph (105 kph), correctly indicated on the speedometer. If the revs are allowed to reach five figures, it was possible to put over 70 mph (112 kph) on the speedo, given a favourable wind and/or gradient.

'For cruising, the bike would lope along tirelessly at a steady 55-60 mph (88-96 kph) with plenty of throttle in reserve. Not so long ago, performance like that would have done credit to a trail bike of 200 cc.'

For 1974 Honda introduced an entirely new 250 cc twin although rather confusingly they stuck to the old CB250 designation. The *Motor Cycle* tester reported: 'The all-new Honda CB250 has a dual personality. Use all the 10,000 rpm in conjunction with the brand new six-speed gearbox and you have an out-and-out sportster. But if you merely want to plonk around town, it's one of the sweetest medium-sized bikes on the market.'

It was followed a year later by Honda's biggest machine up to that time – the super luxury Gold Wing GL1000 designed for the touring rider who wanted a big, comfortable motor cycle that would cruise all day at 70 mph (112 kph) even when laden with pillion passenger and camping gear. Primarily it was aimed at the American market where the massive V-twin Harley-Davidson still

Down in the forest . . . Motor Cycle *tester John Ebbrell puts the SL125 through its off-road paces*

Opposite, top: *the original CB750 of 1969, the best sold superbike of all time*

Opposite, bottom: *the GL1000 Gold Wing was designed for the long distance touring rider*

The massively styled CB250 of 1974. Robust but ungainly compared to the delightful CB72 of a few years earlier

Road cruiser. Motor Cycle tester John Nutting is almost dwarfed by the bulk of the mighty GL1000 Gold Wing of 1975

commanded a big market but it proved surprisingly fast when taken to MIRA and put through the electronic timing trap by the *Motor Cycle* staff. It was the fastest Honda ever tested up to then, with a best one way speed of 130 mph (209 kph) and there-and-back average of 124.6 mph (199.6 kph).

Commenting on the Gold Wing, tester John Nutting wrote: 'Honda's latest and heaviest metal to hit the British market, the GL1000 Gold Wing, is full of surprises. Such as, for example, the fact that the 1000 cc water-cooled four-cylinder engine with shaft-drive is the smoothest, quietest and sweetest unit ever slotted between two wheels. In spite of its weight of 650 lb (295 kg) with a full tank, it steers and handles as well as many 750s. For a machine of its size and stature the Gold Wing will surprise a few speed merchants too. Although obviously not intended as a performance machine, the Wing will see off most big bikes both from a standstill, from which it can reach 60 mph (96 kph) in 4 seconds, as well as higher up the speed range.

'The motorway is the Wing's heaven and the straighter and longer the better. A pity the speed limit allows barely a nudging of the bike's potential. If ever there was a definitive touring machine combining effortless power with stately manners – this is it. At 70 mph (112 kph) in top one is hardly scratching the surface of the Wing's capabilities. Gliding along on a magic carpet, the only sound is of the wind whistling past your helmet.

'First overwhelming impression of the machine is not so much its size (although wheelbase is almost 61 inches/155 cm and if the dummy tank were real, it would hold all of 7 gallons) but the attractiveness of the engine.

'Pulling the car-type choke next to the instruments and pressing the starter button, the engine spins up to 3,000 rpm as the choke mechanism slightly opens the throttles. It will pull almost immediately and within seconds the throttle can be used tentatively. The water-cooling system, pressurised with an overflow tank in the offside of the dummy tank where the emergency kick-start lever is kept ready to be plugged into the rear of the motor, warms up with the aid of a thermostat and within a few minutes, the temperature gauge in the rev counter is at the bottom of the normal range.

'Under load, the engine is perfectly vibrationless. By comparison, the 750 Honda four is uncomfortably buzzy at speed and is more difficult to ride at low speed with its lack of flywheel effect. Here the Gold Wing is a revelation. The only times a suggestion of vibration is felt is on the over-run with a closed throttle and at very low speeds (below 20 mph/32 kph) in top gear when the transmission judders slightly. And with the even firing pulses of the four cylinders and a reasonable-size fly-wheel on the crankshaft, throttle response is smooth and snatch free. Also, by the use of the 300-watt generator as a contra-rotating anti-torque-reaction device, there is none of the side movement when blipping the throttle well known to BMW owners. As a result, engine performance is silky throughout the power range.

'But like all Hondas it is still a top end bike. It pulls from 1,000 rpm and most times no more than 4,000 rpm is enough to fling you forward in a most exciting manner. In fact, even though the handbook recommended no more than 5,000 rpm during the first 600 miles (965 km), this is 88 mph (141 kph) in top gear.

'Power delivery is so easy at this level, however, that it is easy to forget that beyond 5,000 rpm there is a whole new world of excitement.

'Drop the hammer with more than just a few revs from a stop and the rear wheel takes all the punishment. But actually the quickest way is by slipping the super-light clutch. Then, with the engine revving to beyond 8,000, although still producing no more sound than a washing machine at full chat, you're catapulted forward with the impact of a Boeing 747 on take-off.

'There is no real sensation of speed. It's just that sooner or later you need to brake and then you find that the bike is going at an alarming speed.'

The Gold Wing was in fact Honda's first water-cooled motor cycle and also the first with shaft drive. With occasional face-lifts it remained a steady seller for the next decade.

A whole batch of rather ordinary bread-and-butter models were also introduced into the range in 1975 – mainly vertical twins. About the CB360 (powered by a 365 cc engine and featuring a six-speed gearbox and electric starter) the *Motor Cycle* tester said, with commendable frankness: '... when legislators have finally hounded the motor cyclist to the brink of extinction, he will probably be riding something like the Honda CB360 twin.

'It is the bureaucrat's dream. Quiet and unobtrusive as a Swiss watch, reliable as Big Ben,

Gold Wing GL1000

Specification

Engine: 1,000 cc (7261.4 mm) overhead camshaft, water-cooled, opposed flat four. Light-alloy cylinder heads, steel linered cylinders integral with crankcase. Three plain main bearings; plain big-end bearings. Wet sump lubrication. Compression ratio, 9.2 to 1. Four 32-mm Mikuni CV carburettors; paper element air filter. Claimed maximum power, 80 bhp at 7,500 rpm.
Transmission: Inverted-tooth primary chain. Wet, multiplate clutch and five-speed gearbox beneath crankshaft. Final drive by reduction gear from layshaft and cardan shaft. Overall ratios: 11.98, 8.18, 6.39, 5.25 and 4.5 to 1.
Electrical Equipment: Twin coil ignition. 12-volt, 300-watt alternator charging 18-amp-hour battery. 7-in diameter Lucas headlamp with 60/65-watt halogen main bulb. Starter motor; water-temperature gauge; electric fuel gauge; headlamp flasher.
Brakes: Hydraulically-operated 11-in diameter duplex disc front; 11.5-in diameter single rear.
Suspension: Telescopic front fork; pivoted rear fork with five-position spring preload adjustment.
Dimensions: Wheelbase, 60.5 in (153.6 cm); ground clearance, 6 in (15.2 cm).
Kerb Weight: 616 lb (279 kg).
Fuel Capacity: 4.2 gallons (19.1 litres).

Performance

Best One-way Speed: 130 mph (209 kph); dry track, strong tail wind.
Best Standing Quarter-mile: 13.2 sec/103.7 mph (166.8 kph).
Fuel Consumption: 41.6 mpg overall.
Braking Distance: From 30 mph, 29 ft.

Above: *the beautifully engineered flat-four, overhead camshaft engine of the GL1000 Gold Wing of 1975*

Left: *unique feature of the GL1000 Gold Wing is the dummy fuel tank which houses air-filter, tool tray and the electrical components. Petrol is carried in a tank under the seat*

Opposite: *truly King of the Road – the six-cylinder CBX1000 is a real man's motor cycle*

A best-seller of the mid-1970s, the CB360

clean and tidy enough to be parked in the lobby of the Dorchester, comfortable as an easy chair, and a willing starter, it never begs to be ridden fast. That's just as well, for the handling on the open road left plenty to be desired.

'As a result, the CB360 is about as characterless as a real motor cycle can get. True, it performs all of the tasks that the everyday motor cyclist will demand of it, but there's a somewhat bitter aftertaste at the end of each ride.

'It is all very strange. Honda, the world's largest bike manufacturer, introduced the current CB250 and CB360 twins as improved developments with updated styling of the old two-fifty and CB350 which had been going since 1968. They had carved an invincible niche being good all-rounders with sober styling and adequate performance. But the new models were completely new designs in every way, and not all the better for it either.

'The engines, though the same basic layout, with 180-degree crankshafts and single overhead camshafts, were completely modified, too. Major changes were the use of plain bearings for the camshaft, a better oil pump and the moving of the camshaft chain tensioner to the front of the crankcases. The gearbox was given six speeds.

'There is no doubt that the Honda twins are extremely robust units. With the same stroke of 50.6 mm, the difference in capacity is given by

CB360

Specification

Engine: 356 cc (6750.6 mm) overhead camshaft parallel twin. One ball and three roller main bearings; needle-roller big-end bearings. Wet sump lubrication, 4.5 pt (2.5 litres) capacity. Compression ratio, 9.3 to 1. Two 30-cm Keihin CV carburettors; paper-element air filters. Claimed maximum power, 34 bhp at 9,500 rpm.
Transmission: Primary by gears. Wet, multiplate clutch and six-speed gearbox. Chain final drive. Overall ratios: 19.73, 13.81, 10.85, 8.77, 7.62 and 6.83 to 1.
Electrical Equipment: Coil ignition. 12-volt, 130-watt alternator charging 12-amp-hour battery. 6.5-in diameter headlamp with 35/35 main bulb. Starter motor.
Brakes: Hydraulically-operated 10.25-in diameter disc front; 6.5-in diameter drum rear.
Suspension: Telescopic front fork; pivoted rear fork with five-position spring adjustment for load.
Dimensions: Wheelbase, 53.5 in (136 cm); ground clearance, 7 in (17.7 cm).
Kerb Weight: 371 lb (168 kg).
Fuel Capacity: 2.25 gallons (10.2 litres).

Performance

Best One-way Speed: 105 mph (168.9 kph); dry track, strong three-quarter tail wind.
Best Standing Quarter-mile: 15.7 sec/83 mph (133.5 kph).
Fuel Consumption: 85 mpg at 30 mph; 87 mpg at 40 mph; 67 mpg at 50 mph; 56 mpg at 60 mph; 45 mpg at 70 mph.
Braking Distance: From 30 mph, 28 ft 9 in.

Left-hand side view of the CB360

larger, 67-mm diameter, pistons on the 360. This imparts a remarkable capacity for high revving with an equal one for reliability.

'And what a revver! Though the rev-counter red line starts at 9,200 rpm, Honda claim that the engine produces 34 bhp at 9,500 rpm. In practice, however, the power egg would buzz to over 10,000 without any ill-effect and still develop useful urge. Used like this, the CB360 could demonstrate quite a thrilling turn of speed, and the pleasant warble from the upswept exhaust pipes really brought back the days of the racing twins.

'Performance proved to be merely average for the three-fifty class. Top speed through the MIRA trap was a mean 97 mph (156.1 kph), and acceleration 15.7 seconds for the quarter-mile, though this time might have been improved if the gearing had been lowered, for the bike was fairly overgeared and would pull the same speed in fifth as in top.'

Ah, well . . . you cannot win them all! And 1975 turned out to be a relatively bad year for Honda with overall production down from the record 2,132,902 of the previous year to 1,782,448 – the factory's lowest output since 1969 but still an awful lot of motor cycles. The poor figure (every other manufacturer suffered too) was caused by a recession in the American and South East Asian markets.

But one gem of a bike was launched that year

CB400F

Specification

Engine: 408 cc (51 × 50 mm) overhead camshaft transverse, in-line four. Five plain main bearings; plain big-end bearings. Wet sump lubrication 6.2 pt (3.5 litres) capacity. Compression ratio, 9.4 to 1. Four 20-mm Keihin carburettors; paper-element air filter. Claimed maximum power, 37 bhp at 8,500 rpm.
Transmission: Primary by inverted-tooth chain and spur gears. Wet, multiplate clutch and six-speed gearbox. Chain final drive. Overall ratios: 20.9, 13.8, 10.5, 8.5, 7.38 and 6.62 to 1.
Electrical Equipment: Coil ignition. 12-volt, 156-watt alternator charging 12-amp-hour battery. 6.5-in diameter headlamp with 50/35-watt sealed beam unit. Starter motor.
Brakes: Hydraulically-operated 10.5-in diameter disc front; 6.5-in diameter drum rear.
Suspension: Telescopic front fork; pivoted rear fork with five-position spring preload adjustment.
Dimensions: Wheelbase, 54.5 in (138 cm); ground clearance, 6.5 in (16.5 cm).
Kerb Weight: 392 lb (178 kg) with one gallon of fuel.
Fuel Capacity: 3.1 gallons (14.1 litres).

Performance

Best One-way Speed: 105 mph (168.9 kph); dry track, slight tail wind.
Best Standing Quarter-mile: 14.9 sec/87.3 mph (140.4 kph).
Fuel Consumption: 101 mpg at 30 mph; 93 mpg at 40 mph; 82 mpg at 50 mph; 70 mpg at 60 mph; 54 mpg at 70 mph.
Braking Distance: From 30 mph, 29 ft.

Neat and functional – the left-hand side of the delightful little four-cylinder CB400F tested in 1975

Opposite, top: *the flat six prototype for the 'King of Kings' motor cycle. Code-named AOK, it has a car-style alternator that can be seen to the rear of the cylinder bank driven by a skew gear from the camshaft*

Opposite, bottom: *on this CX360 V-twin prototype, code-named A3S 11, water cooling was seen as necessary to cope with impending noise and exhaust emission regulations*

and became an overnight classic as far as European riders were concerned – the delightful little four-cylinder CB400F, a genuine sports model ideally suited to the British market. *Motor Cycle* chief tester John Nutting enthused:

'It cruises at 45 mph (72 kph) with all the serene grace of a Royal Garden Party. It purrs and coos with all the soft innocence of a pair of doves. But drop down two or three gears and gun it and Honda's new CB400 four transforms into a tyre-spinning, screaming 10,000 rpm re-incarnation of a grand prix bike.

'Either way, whether a boulevard bird-puller or boy racer, the CB400F marks an important turning point in the Japanese company's policy. For they have actually gone and done it! Honda have made a super sports bike worthy of the title – in every aspect of its performance as well as its exciting appearance.

'Now I'll agree that in the past I've not been a great Honda lover. But, ever since they first imported what many people regarded as their pace-setters, the ultra-sporty CB72 twins, Honda had diluted the performance and handling features of their bikes to the point of the latest CB250 twins.

'The CB400F changes all that at a stroke. With looks that scream "racer" from every sparkling highlight on those distinctive four-into-one exhaust pipes to the scarlet works-style tank and mini side covers and folding set-back foot-rests, it feels so unarguably *right*, it's almost unbelievable.

'Smooth as a turbine and quiet as any car, the CB400F offers nimble, secure handling whether in dense traffic or wafting down country lanes. It is also very compact and light for a four-cylinder machine. Anyone used to the usual two-fifties should have no trouble with this one.

'Moreover, the performance figures make immensely refreshing reading. Top speed (a mean of two opposing runs at MIRA's test track, remember) is at 104 mph (167 kph), only 1 mph down on the 500 four's, and standing-quarter-mile acceleration of 14.9 seconds is only fractionally down on the bigger model. Such figures are not remarkable in themselves for the 350-400 cc class but they are allied to an economy to make anybody blink twice.

'On a steady throttle at 70 mph (112 kph), it clocked 55 mpg (5.1 litres/100 km) while at 30 mph (47 kph) a fantastic 101 mpg (2.8 litres/100 km) was returned, almost as good as the old CB250. Even driven fast, the CB400F was good. Without the confines of the 70 mph (112 kph) limit, it can sing along at 80-85 mph (128-136 kph) with no more sound than the hiss from the valve gear and even then the consumption still does not drop below 51 mpg (5.5 litres/100 km).

'An unashamed sports bike, the CB400 is bound to carve a position in the market. Those who want the thrills of a compact superbike will find it appealing. It does inevitably have disadvantages for the two-up touring rider, mainly due to its small size and pillion footrests mounted to

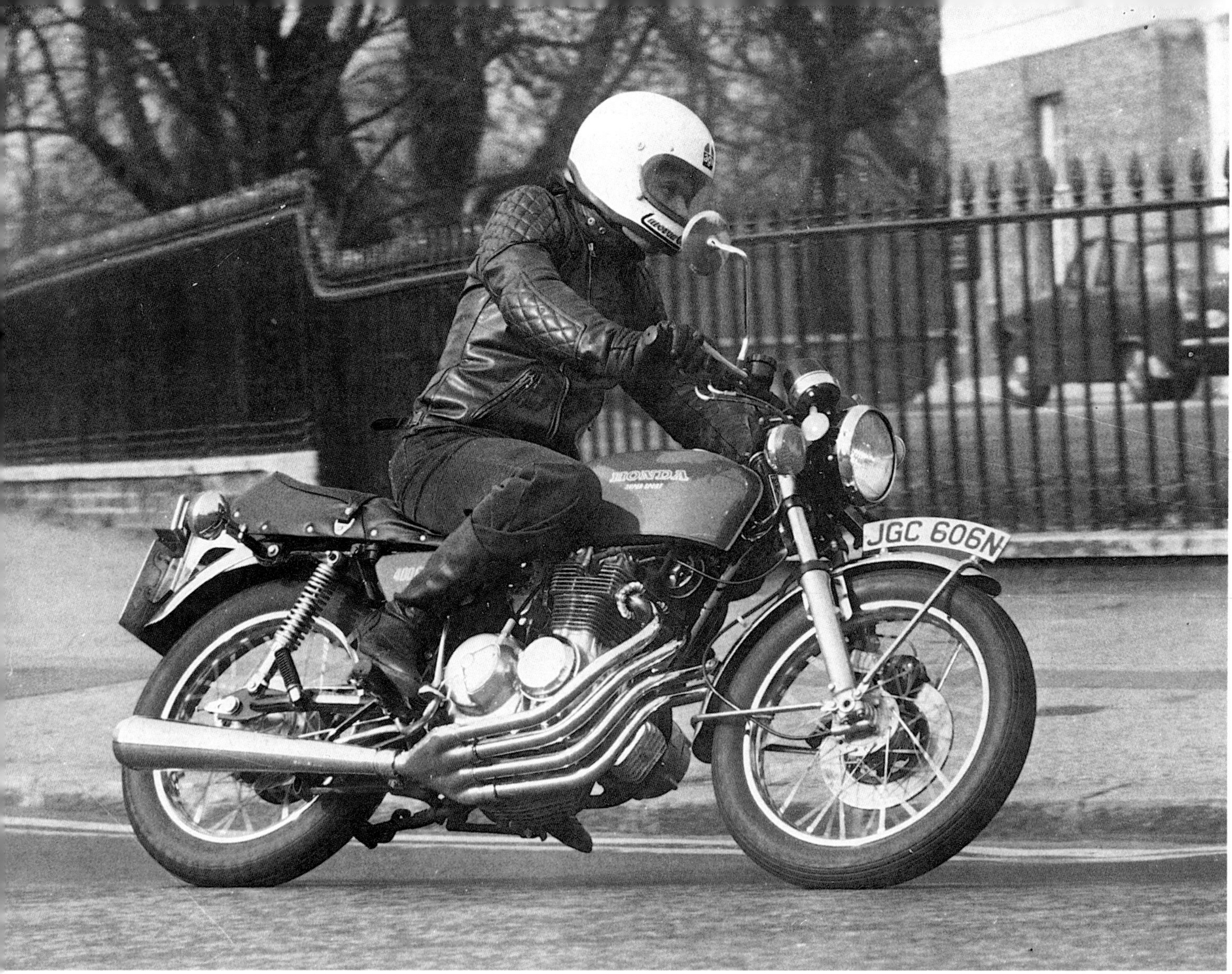
HONDA
JGC 606N

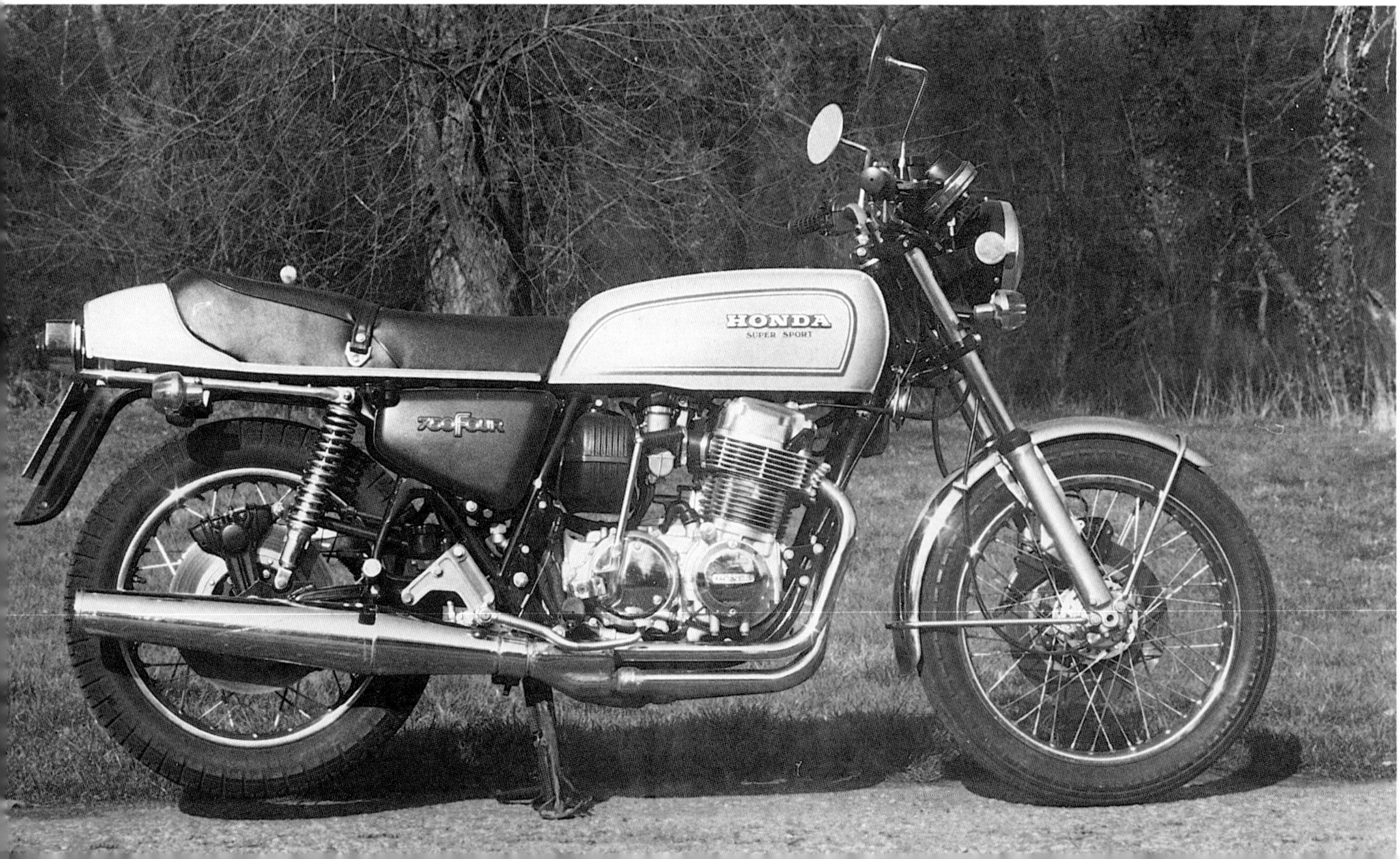
HONDA
SUPER SPORT

Opposite, top: *little racer. To Motor Cycle tester John Nutting, the CB400F was a gem. Note the impressive four-into-one exhaust*

Opposite, bottom: *the CB750F of 1976 was fast but heavy and lacked the style of both earlier and later Honda seven-fiftys*

Above: *one of the neatest Hondas of all time – the CB750F2 of the late 1970s*

the rear fork.

'But it will hit the other three-fifties and four-hundreds hard. As exciting and sporty as a 350 Yamaha or 400 two-stroke Kawasaki but with the KZ400 Kawa's or 350 Morini's economy plus luxury finish and comfort, the CB400F has just got to be a winner.'

It sold well in the UK but strangely not in North America and was phased out after just two years in favour of a twin. Filling the capacity gap a 500 cc twin and a 550 cc four were added to the range and the good old SL125 was replaced by the XL125. In 1976 the CB750 was updated and marketed as the Super Sports CB750F with an eye-catching yellow finish.

Said *Motor Cycle*: 'The new 750 cc Honda four is a jet! With the best all-round timed figures for a seven-fifty, the Super Sports CB750F is the quickest machine in its class.'

Best one way speed clocked was 125 mph (201 kph) with a mean speed of 122 mph (196 kph) for two runs in opposite directions. In fact, the bike was a stop-gap model and was replaced in 1977 by the vastly improved CB750F2 with improved styling and the five-spoke Comstar wheels so familiar today.

Honda had been busy – and in 1978 launched a succession of impressive machines. Most sensational and certainly one of the most impressive motor cycles of all time was the incredible six-cylinder 1,047 cc CBX, a super sports model with a top speed potential around the 140 mph (225 kph) mark. The model was announced at a press conference in Japan in December 1977 and was put through its impressive paces by *Motor Cycle* in April 1978. Wrote chief-tester John Nutting:

'When the rumours of Honda's big six first broke last December, they seemed too fantastic to be true. After all, an across-the-frame 1,000 cc six was only the sort of bike you dreamed about! And with the top manufacturers moving toward more sane designs like compact fours, a six went beyond the bounds of credibility.

'But here it is in the flesh. And riding it around normal roads, the CBX proves to be every bit as incredible as when I first rode one of the prototypes at the Suzuka racing circuit in Japan late last year. Despite its, at first, absurdly monstrous appearance it is very manageable once on the move. It steers beautifully and with an engine of boundless potency and flexibility is a real joy to ride.

'It is also an amalgam of many things desired by the sporting rider. Tapered seat and tank mean that it is slim where its pilot sits and has an excellent riding position. And almost mira-

CBX

culously the machine has the ground clearance of a racing bike.

'Miraculously because when sitting astride this majestic machine for the first time those six cylinders rustling and panting for action is one of the most breathtaking and intimidating sights available to the road rider.

'Snap the throttle. It's light and the engine sings in immediate response with a metallic and husky shriek. There is hardly a rattle from the bike either, it is so uncannily smooth. It is then that you begin to believe that the Honda CBX is at the crossroads of reality and fantasy – designers have produced their dream in the most practical form possible. As such, the CBX is a brilliant achievement.

'Once into its stride, there is nothing to touch the bike for drag-racer acceleration. Imprudent use of the throttle can lift the front wheel or spin the back wheel. Hang on and the CBX catapults like a ballistic missile.

'There is no disputing the engine's claimed 105 bhp at 9,000 rpm. More than that, the way the power creeps up so relentlessly makes the CBX devastating. With a rev range that spreads from 800 rpm to the red line at 10,300 rpm there is nothing it cannot do. Wind it up in any gear and in fractions of a second it can be whistling along

Opposite and above: *sheer power! The six-cylinder CBX1000 created a sensation when it was launched in 1977*

CBX1000

Specification

Engine: 1,047 cc (64.5 × 53.4 mm) double overhead camshaft, in-line, four-stroke six, across the frame. Four valves per cylinder. Seven plain main bearings; plain big-end bearings. Wet sump, 9.7 pt (5.5 litres) capacity. Compression ratio, 9.3 to 1. Six 28-mm Keihin CV carburettors. Claimed maximum power, 105 bhp at 9,000 rpm.
Transmission: Morse-type chain to countershaft. Spur gears to wet, multiplate clutch and five-speed gearbox. Overall ratios, 12.86, 9.26, 7.36, 6.35 and 5.49 to 1.
Electrical Equipment: Capacitor discharge ignition. 12-volt, 240-watt alternator charging 14-amp-hour battery. 60/55-watt H4 halogen headlamp. Starter motor, headlamp flasher.
Brakes: Hydraulically-operated discs, twin 10.75-in diameter front, single 11.75-in diameter rear.
Suspension: Telescopic front fork. Pivoted rear fork and suspension units with five-position spring preload adjustment. Also with two-position compression damping and three-position rebound damping adjustment.
Dimensions: Wheelbase, 59 in (149.8 cm); ground clearance, 7.5 in (19 cm).
Kerb Weight: 558 lb (253 kg) including one gallon of fuel.
Fuel Capacity: 4.4 gallons (20 litres).

Performance

Best One-way Speed: 139.2 mph (224 kph); dry track, light westerly wind.
Best Standing Quarter-mile: 11.75 sec/116.3 mph (187.1 kph).
Fuel Consumption: 65 mpg at 30 mph; 54 mpg at 40 mph; 58 mpg at 50 mph; 63 mpg at 60 mph; 38 mpg at 70 mph.
Braking Distance: From 30 mph, 27.5 ft.

Six cylinders, six carburettors, double overhead camshafts and four-valves per cylinder. An engineer's dream come true! An overhead view of the CBX1000

at very illegal speeds. The British legal limit is reached in 4.5 seconds from rest, while just a flick of the wrist in third will take you from a traffic crawl to over 100 mph (160 kph) in the blink of an eye.

'Top gear is good for over 140 mph (225 kph) so at normally legal speeds there is ample room for playing with the gearbox, which changes slickly and silently, and certainly better than most other Hondas.

'At the test strip the big Honda clocked a mean two-way top speed of 136.5 mph (219.6 kph) with a best one-way of 139.2 mph (224 kph). The CBX is also the quickest accelerating machine we have ridden. With a standing quarter-mile in 11.75 seconds and showing 116.3 mph (187.1 kph) at the end, the CBX is in the same class as many of the Street-class drag racers. Yet the bike will happily trickle along at 11 mph (17 kph) in top.

'The Honda CBX is probably the most magnificent piece of machinery to hit the road. It is indulgent, unnecessary and beautiful! From the looks it got, car drivers and motor cyclists alike, the CBX is perfect for posing. But it is a poser's bike with the punch of a sledgehammer.'

Technically the engine was a masterpiece. There were four valves per cyclinder (24 in all!), double overhead camshafts, six 28 mm Keihin carburettors plus a five-speed gearbox. Power of the standard model was 105 bhp at 9,000 rpm – so high that a detuned model had to be built for West Germany which had imposed a 100 bhp limit for motor cycles!

Opposite, bottom: *Honda broke new ground with the unusual water-cooled V-twin CX500 introduced in 1978*

Above: *a travelling marshall swings a CX500 around the TT course in the Isle of Man*

CX500

Specification

Engine: 497 cc (78 × 52 mm) water cooled, ohv, 80-degree V-twin with four valves per cylinder. Two plain main bearings; plain big-end bearings. Wet sump, 6.5 pt (3.7 litres) capacity. Compression ratio, 10 to 1. Two 35-mm Keihin CV carburettors; paper-element air filter. Claimed maximum power, 50 bhp at 9,000 rpm.

Transmission: Primary spur gears. Wet, multiplate clutch and five-speed gearbox. Final drive by shaft and spiral bevel gears. Overall ratios: 18.9, 12.8, 8.9, 7.96 and 6.45 to 1.

Electrical Equipment: Capacitor-discharge ignition. 12-volt, 170-watt alternator charging 14-amp-hour battery. 6.5-in headlamp with 60/55-watt halogen main bulb. Starter motor, headlamp flasher.

Brakes: Hydraulically-operated dual 9.5-in diameter disc front; 6.5-in diameter rod-operated drum rear.

Suspension: Telescopic front fork; pivoted rear fork with two FVQ dampers and five-position spring preload adjustment.

Dimensions: Wheelbase, 58.75 in (149.2 cm); ground clearance, 7 in (17.7 cm).

Kerb Weight: 467 lb (212 kg) including one gallon of fuel.

Fuel Capacity: 3.7 gallons (16.8 litres) including 6 pt reserve.

Performance

Best One-way Speed: 117.7 mph (189.4 kph); dry track, strong tail wind.

Best Standing Quarter-mile: 14.5 sec/92.5 mph (148.8 kph).

Fuel Consumption: 64 mpg at 30 mph; 63 mpg at 40 mph; 59 mpg at 50 mph; 52 mpg at 60 mph; 44 mpg at 70 mph.

Braking Distance: From 30 mph, 28 ft.

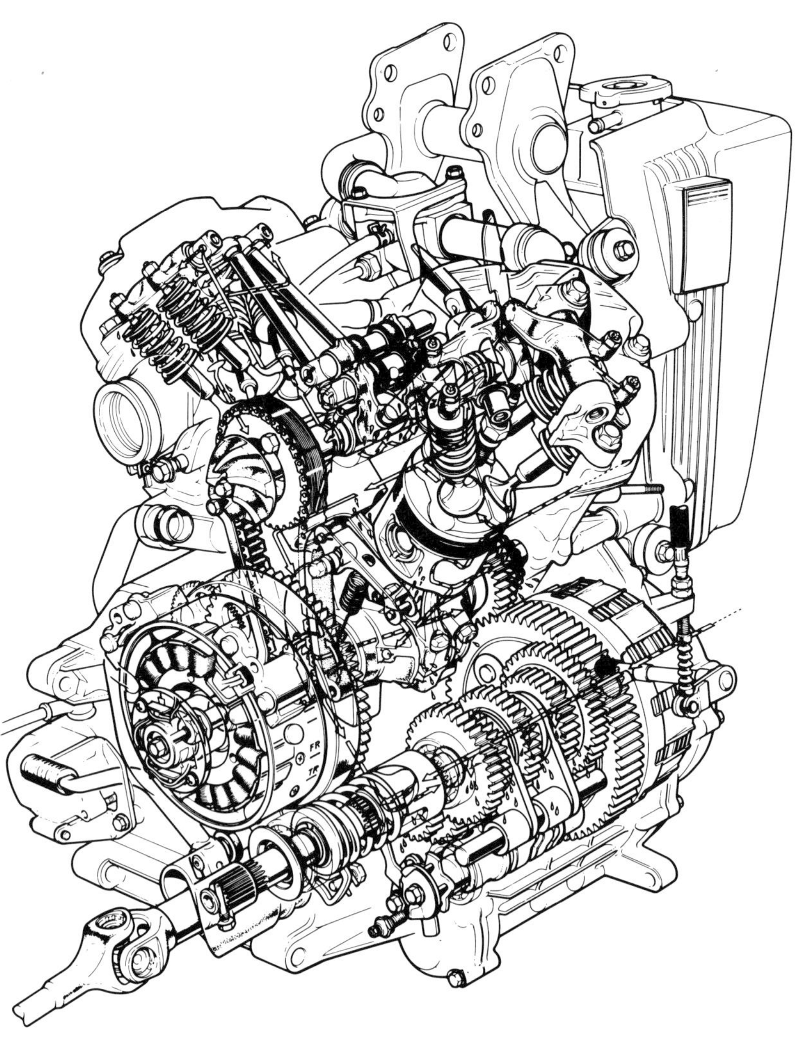

Equally interesting and in some ways more technically surprising was Honda's new offering for the 500 cc class – the CX500 which was also marketed in 1978. For while the CBX was clearly inspired by the six-cylinder racers of the 1960s the CX500 was powered by a completely new engine: a water-cooled V-twin set across the frame so that the cylinder heads stuck out on both sides just below the fuel tank.

With shaft-drive it was designed for the man who wanted a trouble free commuter-cum-tourer and as such it impressed *Motor Cycle Weekly* chief tester John Nutting: '... not only is the bike a pace-setter in rider comfort, handling, performance and quietness but it manages to raise the ease of maintenance for a Japanese machine to a new high.

'All this is the result of careful and logical engineering that has resulted in a water-cooled, V-twin with four valves per cylinder and shaft-drive, a simple spine frame and composite steel and light alloy wheels with tubeless tyres. It is without doubt a motor cycle of the 1980s ...'

During the speed testing it proved surprisingly fast ... 'With the rider flat on the tank, the CX500 clocked a mean of 110.4 mph (177.6 kph) at just over 9,000 rpm in top, running up to 117 mph (188.3 kph) with a strong tail wind. Standing start quarter-mile figures were slightly better than the CB550 at 14.5 seconds and a terminal speed of 92.5 mph (148.8 kph).'

Unfortunately for Honda the early CX500s suffered from cam-chain tensioner and big-end problems but despite these the machine proved to be a best seller.

For a while in the late 1970s Honda offered a novelty – a CB400 twin fitted with Hondamatic transmission. Like the Honda car system this is not fully automatic but has a gear pedal to select low or high ratio. However, the bike could be ridden as an automatic by simply leaving it in top and letting the torque converter do the rest.

Naturally there was a power less but Honda thought that commuting riders would be willing to sacrifice performance for ease of riding – no declutching, no gear-changing, just twist the throttle and go. But while this was wanted on smaller, utility machines such as Honda's own best selling step-throughs, the buyer looking for a bigger machine just was not interested and the CB400A simply did not sell and gradually faded away.

Celebrating ten years in production the good old four-cylinder seven-fifty was given yet another face-lift, including a completely revised engine with double overhead camshafts, changed bore and stroke and power upped from the 70 bhp of the previous model to 77 bhp – enough to propel the machine at an average of 127.6 mph (205.3 kph) during tests with a best one-way speed of 135 mph (217.2 kph).

Writing about the newcomer, designation CB750KZ, the *Motor Cycle Weekly* tester said in January 1979: 'Honda's new 750 four is almost a dream motor cycle. It's as if Honda, when considering the specification for the replacement for their ten-year-old single overhead camshaft four, built every possible desirable feature into the bike.'

In 1979 Honda also launched a 650 cc single overhead camshaft four to fill the gap between their 550 and the new 750. And later in the year came an improved version of the Gold Wing – the GL1000KZ. Twelve months later this was replaced by the GL1100 with the engine enlarged to 1,085 cc.

Filling the gap between the constantly updated CB750 and the six-cylinder CBX, Honda introduced the four-cylinder CB900 and this model certainly impressed *Motor Cycle Weekly* tester Stewart Boroughs in October 1979: 'Gorgeous looks – absolutely mouth-watering, in particular the upswept exhausts and mirror finish of aluminium-alloy engine castings, crisp acceleration from the silky-smooth mill which will maintain three-figure speeds with nonchalence, complimented by a clunkless gear-change and comfortable riding position.

'Electrics, too, are top notch with the headlight, like the gear-change, arguably the best yet experienced on a Honda. The roles of racer and roadster are poles apart, but what you cannot get away from on any motor cycle is its "heart" – in the nine-hundred a 16-valve, transverse four-cylinder that produces an abundance of power, peaking at 95 bhp at 9,000 rpm.

'The motor spins readily and freely up to the 9,500 blood-line with the minimum of high frequency fuzz blurring the rapidly diminishing images in the mirrors. No kick in the seat either for power delivery is exceptionally smooth.

'Lifting the throttles gives instant response and up to 4,000 rpm the nine-hundred is as smooth as the CBX six. It is a top gear bike with oodles of torque that the tourist needs and almost makes

Opposite, top: *bristling with interesting technical features, the water-cooled, V-twin CX500 engine has four-valves per cylinder, operated by short pushrods and a five-speed gearbox positioned alongside the engine with shaft drive to the rear wheel*

Opposite, bottom: *in the late 1970s Honda offered the CB400AT with two-speed Hondamatic gearbox*

Below: *CB900F four-cylinder, sports roadster of 1979 with European styling*

CB900FZ

Specification

Engine: 902 cc (64.5 × 69 mm) double overhead camshaft, 16-valve in-line, transverse four. Five plain main bearings; plain big-end bearings. Wet sump, 8 pt (4.5 litres) capacity. Compression ratio, 8.8 to 1. Four 32-mm Keihin CV carburettors. Claimed maximum power, 95 bhp at 9,000 rpm.
Transmission: Inverted tooth chain and gear primary drive. Wet, multiplate clutch and five-speed gearbox. Chain final drive. Overall ratios: 13.38, 9.45, 7.35, 6.13 and 5.28 to 1.
Electrical Equipment: Transistorised ignition.12-volt, 260-watt alternator charging 14-amp-hour battery. 6.5-in Stanley headlamp with 60/55-watt halogen main bulb. Starter motor; headlamp flasher.
Brakes: Hydraulically-operated discs, twin 10.8-in diameter front, single 11.6-in diameter rear.
Suspension: Telescopic front fork with air adjustment; pivoted rear fork and FVQ shock absorbers with four-way adjustable damping and five-position spring preload adjustment.
Dimensions: Wheelbase, 60.5 in (153.6 cm); ground clearance, 6 in (15.2 cm).
Kerb Weight: 538 lb (244 kg) including one gallon fuel.
Fuel Capacity: 4.4 gallons (20 litres) including one gallon fuel.

Performance

Best One-way Speed: 128.9 mph (207.4 kph); warm, dry, still air.
Best Standing Quarter-mile: 12.61 sec/108.44 mph (173.51 kph).
Fuel Consumption: 65 mpg at 30 mph; 64 mpg at 40 mph; 62 mpg at 50 mph; 57 mpg at 60 mph; 45 mpg at 70 mph.
Braking Distance: From 30 mph, 29 ft.

the gearbox obsolete. Which is a shame really for the cog-swopper is the best I have encountered on a Honda.

'The gear-change is the same as that on its smaller stablemate the CB750KZ (the two models share the same sturdy, full loop frame), a linkage system positive and backlash-free and mounted on one of a pair of long alloy castings which support the pillion footrests and locates the rider's high-mounted folding pegs nicely beneath the seat of his riding suit.

'When tested in January this year, the 77 bhp CB750KZ was a flyer, the fastest in its class, breaking the beams at the MIRA test track near Nuneaton with a shattering mean speed of 127.64 mph (205.41 kph).

'Sucking through 2 mm larger Keihin carburettors, with 32 mm chokes, the lighter CB900FZ (lighter than the four-into-four CB750KZ because of the gorgeous, mellow, big-bore four-into-two exhaust) ran an aggregate of east/west runs of 128.4 mph (206.64 kph). The runs were near-identical either way and the highest speed reached on the day was 129.8 mph (208.89 kph).

'Although there is little between the two in out-and-out performance, the nine-hundred has two marked advantages. It is more relaxing to ride and has a greater spread of power and torque over the seven-fifty which we found did not turn

Getting down to it. Road tester Graham Sanderson swings the CB900F into a corner

on its form until 5,500 rpm was shown on the dial.'

The faithful CB200, 250 and 400 models had been updated at regular intervals during the past two decades but a very welcome newcomer was added in 1980 – the single-cylinder CB250RS. Previously the single-pot quarter-litre Hondas had all been trail bikes but the RS was an out-and-out sports roadster.

Cheaper, lighter and to many eyes more attractive than the rather massively-built CB twins the RS had praise heaped on it by *Motor Cycle Weekly* road test editor Graham Sanderson: 'If there was a prize for the most sensible motor cycle of the year then the Honda CB250RS single would certainly be on the leaderboard. After all a machine which achieves nearly 90 mph (154 kph), a frugal 90 mpg (3.14 litres/100 km) and at a thrifty £759 is one of the cheapest quarter-litre motor cycles available, cannot fail to gain many friends in the overpriced, inflatory age in which we live.'

But it is the big bikes that catch the attention and gain a company publicity and Honda certainly did that when they launched the race-bred CB1100R in 1981. This machine was a production racer virtually ready for the track with clip-on handlebars and streamlined cowling. Finished in white and red it was a real eye-catcher, and at just over £4,000 it was the most expensive Honda motor cycle ever offered on the British market. It recorded a mean of two runs at 136.6 mph (219.8 kph) with a best one-way speed of 138.2 mph (22.4 kph) – virtually the same as the CBX.

Fuel consumption was enough to make an oil sheik smile, averaging out at 34.8 mpg (8.12 litres/100 km) and dropping to 27.8 mpg (10.16 litres/100 km) when ridden hard!

Later that year Honda up-dated the incredible six-cylinder CBX. Called the B model, the 1981 version had Honda's new single-unit Pro Link rear suspension and a comprehensive touring-type fairing with windscreen. It was nowhere near as fast as the original naked sports model and it seemed a shame to demote such a wonderful engine to a mundane touring role.

But the bike that had the most written about it in 1981 was without a doubt the first turbo-charged machine to go into production – the CX 500 Turbo. At first thought, the ugly-duckling twin-cylinder V-twin CX seemed a strange machine to turbocharge but there is no doubt the bike was a success and under long-term test conditions it proved surprisingly trouble free.

After putting the pros and cons for turbo power the *Motor Cycle Weekly* road test team wrote: . . . 'the dominant sensation of riding the Turbo is one of extreme smoothness. The eerie silence and rapidity with which it beams into three-figure speeds is a totally new experience for

Street racer. The super-sports CB1100R was a limited edition production racing machine that made friends for Honda around the world

Above: *naked and unashamed – the CB1100R minus fairing, seat and tank*

the motor cyclist. You literally would not know that the revs were nearing the 9,000 red-line unless you glanced down at the machine's extensive cockpit instrumentation.'

Acceleration was impressive, the Turbo covering the standing start quarter-mile in 13.2 seconds with a terminal speed of 102 mph (164 kph) which is on a par with a good seven-fifty but top speed at around 120 mph (193 kph) was not so impressive and neither was the fuel consumption – just 31 mpg (9.11 litres/100 km) overall, dropping to 22 mpg (12.84 litres/100 km) when ridden hard. Price was roughly double that of the standard CX500 at £3,350.

Less than a year later the company launched an equally eye-catching CX500 variant – the CX500EC Eurosport. As the name implies this was a sports version of old faithful and it was certainly one of the most attractive machines that Honda have ever produced.

In a road test dated August 1982 *Motor Cycle Weekly* described it as 'stunningly attractive', but powered by the same 50 bhp engine as the original model its performance did not match its looks, although it remains in the range as a thoroughly worthwhile motor cycle.

Now Honda are poised to launch a range of high performance two-strokes. For close on 30 years the company concentrated on four-stroke engines but in the 1970s they had to develop high performance strokers to succeed in moto cross.

CX500 Turbo

Specification

Engine: 497 cc (78 × 52 mm) twin cylinder, water-cooled, ohv V-twin. Plain main bearings and big-ends. Compression ratio, 7.2 to 1. Turbocharger with wastegate. Dual map programmed computerised fuel injection system. Wet sump lubrication, 6.2 pt (3.5 litres) capacity. Claimed maximum power, 82 bhp at 8,000 rpm.
Transmission: Primary spur gears. Wet, multiplate clutch and five-speed gearbox. Shaft final drive. Overall ratios: 15.88, 10.89, 8.13, 6.58 and 5.67 to 1.
Electrical Equipment: Transistorised ignition. 12-volt, 240-watt alternator charging 14-amp-hour battery. Rectangular halogen 60/55-watt headlamp. Starter motor; quartz clock; turbo boost readout; fuel and temperature gauges.
Brakes: Hydraulically-operated twin disc front; single disc rear.
Suspension: Air-assisted anti-dive telescopic front fork; pivoted rear fork with single monoshock Pro-Link suspension system.
Dimensions: Wheelbase, 59 in (149.8 cm).
Kerb Weight: 560 lb (254 kg).
Fuel Capacity: 4.4 gallons (20 litres).

Performance

Best One-way Speed: 119.25 mph (191.91 kph).
Best Standing Quarter-mile: 13.2 sec/102 mph (164.1 kph).
Fuel Consumption: 30.7 mpg overall; at constant 50 mph, 44 mpg.

Opposite, bottom: *surely one of the best styled Hondas of all time – the impressive CX500 Turbo*

Below: *rear suspension systems have made great strides in recent years. This underneath picture of the CX500 Turbo shows the Pro-Link system with a single, centrally-mounted unit, developed by Honda*

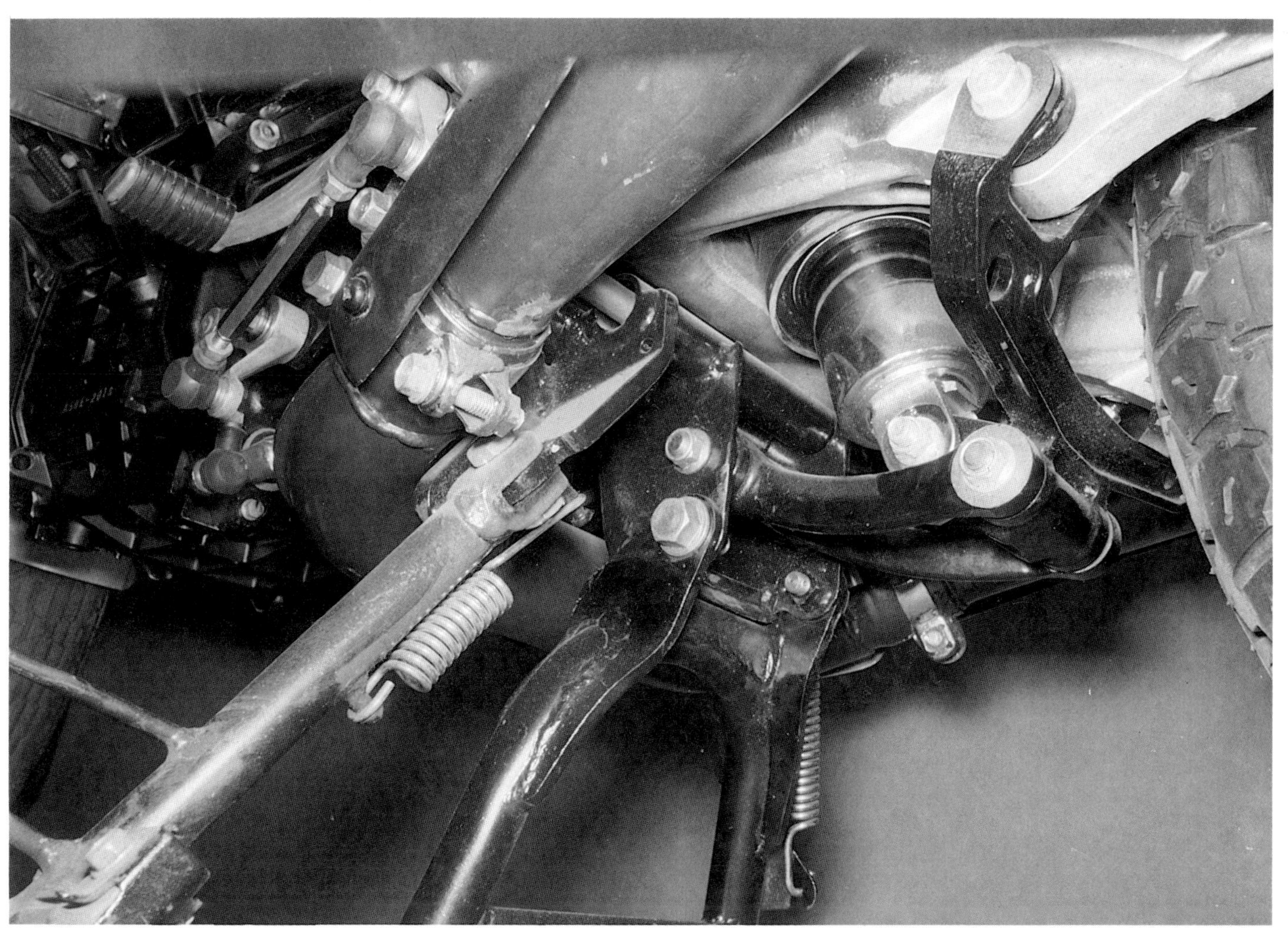

Above and opposite: *broadening the appeal of their machines Honda offer some in American-style Chopper or Custom guise. These photographs are of the CX500C. Features include a smaller tank, high rise handlebars, extended fork, smaller rear wheel and a stepped seat*

A 100 cc roadster followed and when the company were forced to switch from the NR500 to the three-cylinder two-stroke NS500 to achieve success in grand prix road racing the obvious move was to capitalise on the opportunity and to market high performance two-strokes to rival the very successful 250 cc LC Yamaha and RG Suzuki. Sure enough, early in 1983 Honda announced that they were to market an NS-style three-cylinder 250 cc two-stroke sports model.

That then is a brief look, mainly through the eyes of the road testers of *Motor Cycle* and *Motor Cycle Weekly*. It has to be brief for during the company's first 30 years of production they produced no less than 43 million motorcycles – 43,139, 143 to be precise!

HONDA
CX500C

Return to Road Racing

Following Honda's decision to withdraw from world championship road racing at the end of the 1967 season, 15 years were to pass before the factory won another grand prix. The man who followed in Mike Hailwood's wheeltracks to achieve this historic success was Freddie Spencer, a quiet spoken American who won the 500 cc class of the 1982 Belgian Grand Prix in his first season of classic racing.

In fact Honda's return to racing was a gradual affair. In a way it started just three years after that dramatic 1967 withdrawal when the factory entered a team of race-kitted CB750 four-cylinder machines in the Daytona 200. The idea was to boost sales in the American market and it worked, for veteran American Dick Mann rode a coolly calculated race to outlast the considerable factory opposition and win the Florida classic for Honda.

But this was a one-off and it was really the efforts of the factory's British and Continental importers that coaxed Honda back into racing – via production machine and endurance events.

In Britain Honda's name was kept on the racing map with success in the TT by Dealer teams competing in the production events. They scored a notable double in 1971 with Chester dealer Bill Smith winning the 250 cc class and John Williams the 500 cc. A year later Williams took the 250 cc class and in 1973 Smith was victorious on the 500 cc machine.

Two years later the factory in Japan produced their first works engine for five years. The 750 cc unit was prepared for John and Charlie Williams to race in the Belgian Liège and French Bol D'or 24-hour endurance events. The machine had crankcases similar to the CB500 roadster but the rest was very much a works effort. Bore and stroke were 65 × 56.4 mm with the primary and camshaft drives by gears. Two inlet and one exhaust valve per cylinder were used. The whole machine only weighed 340 lb (154 kg), considerably lighter than other endurance machines. Sadly the future of the new project was marred when Japanese tester Morio Sumiya was killed while practicing on one of the new machines at Le Mans. This tragedy coupled with the fact that the factory felt the engine was not strong enough for

Dick Mann has a clear lead on the Honda CB750 in the 1970 Daytona 200 miler. He went on to win the race at an average speed of 102.69 mph (165.26 kph)

SPEEDWAY
DAYTONA
DAYTONA USA

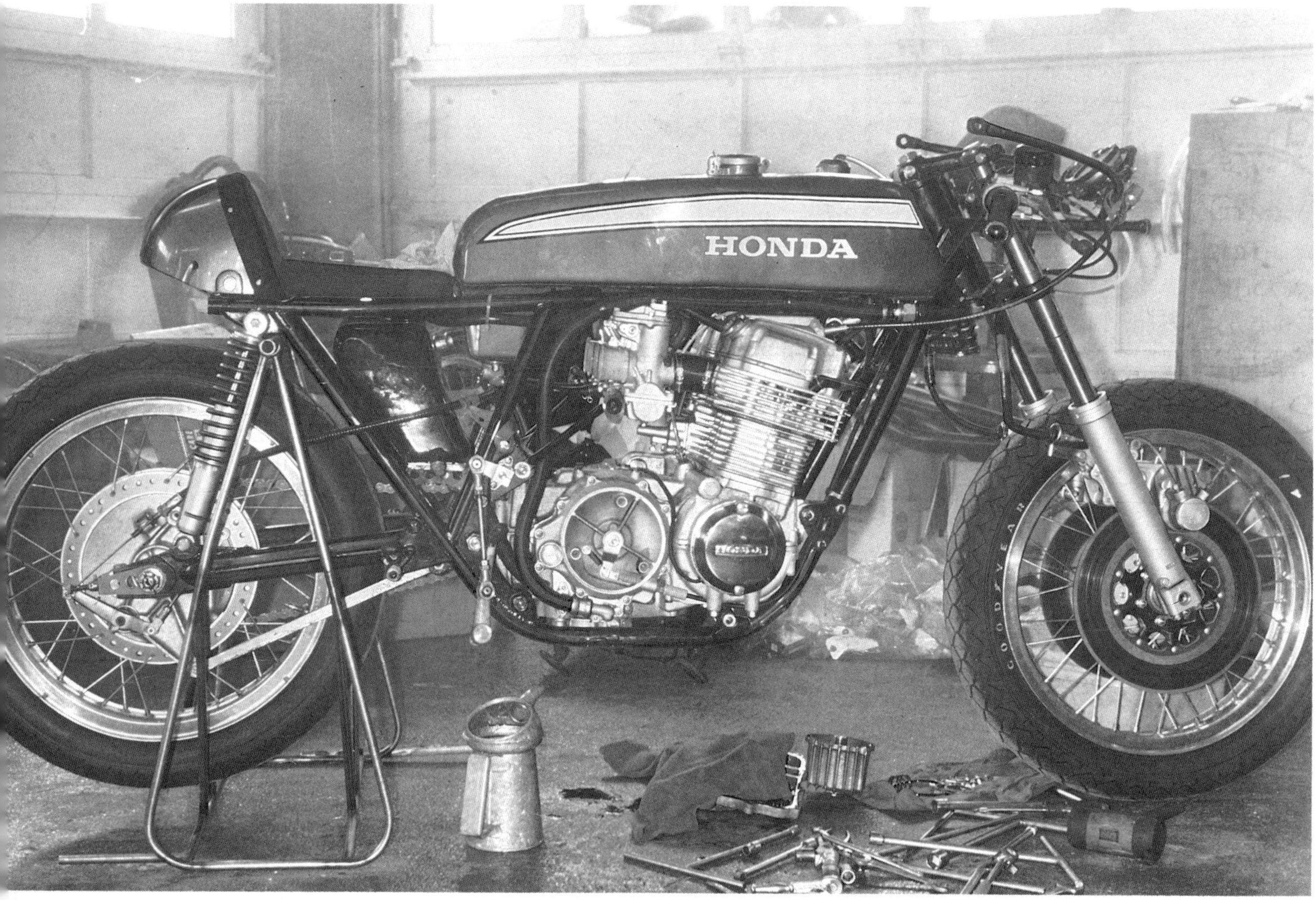
HONDA

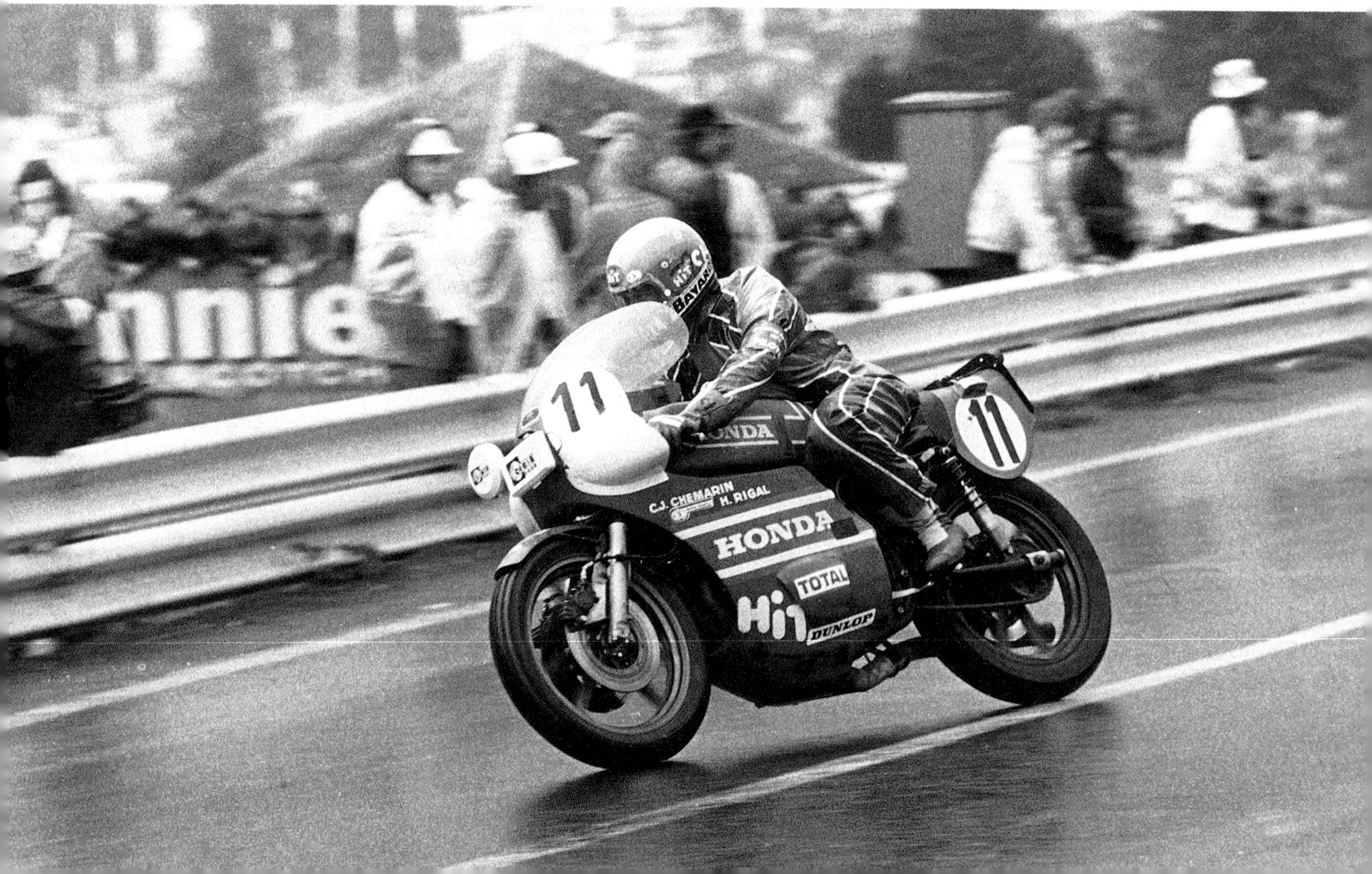
11
HONDA
C.J. CHEMARIN
H. RIGAL
HONDA
TOTAL
DUNLOP
11

endurance racing led to the abandonment of the project.

Despite those setbacks the appetite of some of the older members of Honda's Research and Development had been whetted. They longed for the glory days of the 1960s when Honda dominated the grand prix scene and through their Racing Services Corporation and Honda France they launched a strong attack on the FIM's Coupe d'Endurance series. Never in their wildest dreams could they have realised the success it was going to bring them as they dominated the championship for the next five years.

This domination started in 1976 with the new team setting their sights firmly on two targets: to win the championship and also the prestigious French Bol d'Or race at Le Mans. At the end of the five-round championship series they had achieved both aims, winning every race.

They used 941 cc double-overhead camshaft four-strokes with four valves per cylinder. The first race in the championship at the Italian Mugello circuit was the closest of the series. Frenchmen Jean-Claude Chemarin and Christian Leon gave Honda their first success but it was a mighty close thing. After 191 laps second-placed Pentti Korhonen and Christian Estrosi on a works Ducati and third-placed Jacques Luc and Alain Vial riding a 1000 cc Kawasaki all finished on the same lap.

Britain's Charlie Williams and Stan Woods had no such problems around Montjuich Park in Barcelona where they finished four laps in front of Chemarin and Leon after a record breaking ride.

That was nothing to the 200 miles (320 km) that separated winner Leon and Chemarin from second-placed Daniel Rouge and Christian Huguet at the next round at the Belgian Spa circuit after leaders Woods and Williams had dropped out after 16 hours.

Another Briton, Alex George, who plenty will be written about later, was drafted into the team in place of the injured Leon to team with Chemarin for the all important Bol d'Or. He justified his selection by helping the Frenchman win the race but only after a hard battle. Yvon Duhamel and Jean-Francois Balde, riding a works Kawasaki, led the race for the first 10 hours but then crashed.

Huguet and Roger Ruiz gave Honda a clean sweep by winning the final round at Thruxton in England with Chemarin and Pat Evans second. That gave Honda the manufacturer's title and put Chemarin top of the riders points table. There was no doubt that Honda were back in business.

At Honda UK's headquarters in London plans were being formulated to enter the fray alongside the French-based team. In January 1977 it was announced they were to enter a team in the Coupe

Opposite, top: *naked as a jay bird, the Daytona winning Honda CB750 that brought the company their first success on their return to racing*

Opposite, bottom: *picking a line through the puddles at La Source hairpin, Jean-Claude Chemarin races towards the start and finish on the works Honda*

Above: *Christian Leon pilots the 750 cc Honda to yet another Coupe d'Endurance victory at the 1976 Liège 24 hour race at Spa*

Above: the 1977 998 cc Endurance Honda with a reported power output of 125 bhp and a dry weight of 383 lb (174 kg)

Opposite, top: Phil Read trying all he knows to race through Ballacraine during his ill fated chase on the 888 cc Honda of Mike Hailwood in the 1978 Formula One TT on the Isle of Man

Opposite, lower: Jean-Claude Chemarin on route to clinching the 1978 Coupe d'Endurance title on the Honda RCB 997 cc machine by finishing second in the final round at Brands Hatch

d'Endurance championship and that they were going to sponsor a British 125 cc Honda championship for their new single-cylinder two-stroke 25 bhp machines. The successful duo of Woods and Williams were joined by Geoff Barry and Tony Rutter to ride the endurance machines while changes were also being made by the championship-winning French squad. Michael Rougerie was signed up while Rene Guili and Roger Ruiz were given the sack. The machines were improved with the capacity increased to 998 cc and an anti-dive system fitted to the front forks.

Despite all this news Honda UK dropped the bombshell of the season when they announced at the beginning of May they had signed seven-times world champion Phil Read to ride for them at the TT. They told the stunned press that Read, winner of six TT races, would ride a factory-prepared 820 cc four-cylinder machine in the new Formula 1 race – and the start of a fairy tale return by both the man and machine to the Isle of Man had begun.

Fans' opinions were split about the return of Read who had criticised the safety of the Mountain circuit, and vowed, after the 1972 races, that he would never return. Some TT course marshals threatened a boycott if he rode but the Auto-Cycle Union and the Isle of Man Tourist Board rubbed their hands in glee because the return of Honda and the controversial Mr Read meant a bumper race week in June.

Typically the former world champion brushed aside all criticism and won the race for Honda but almost typically again, his victory had to include a sniff of controversy. The race was shortened to four laps because of pouring rain and Honda UK's team manager, Gerald Davison, heard from ACU officials of the possible abandonment of the last lap before the official announcement. So, as Read pulled in for his second fuel stop at the end of the third lap, Davison waved him on while second placed Roger Nicholls, riding a 862 cc Ducati, stopped to refuel. However, it is doubtful if Nicholls who finished 38.4 seconds adrift, could have mounted a serious last lap challenge because he was suffering from a painful hand injury sustained in a practice crash. To complete a memorable week for Honda, Lancastrian Alan Jackson won the Formula 2 race and John Kidson the Formula 3.

Spurred on by their success and by falling sales of machines to the younger end of the market, Honda UK again produced a master stroke when they signed up 21-year-old Ron Haslam to ride one of their 840 cc machines for the supporting Formula 1 race at the British Grand Prix at Silverstone. The Langley Mill rider had a tremendous following among Britain's younger fans with his tearaway style. He had just finished second to

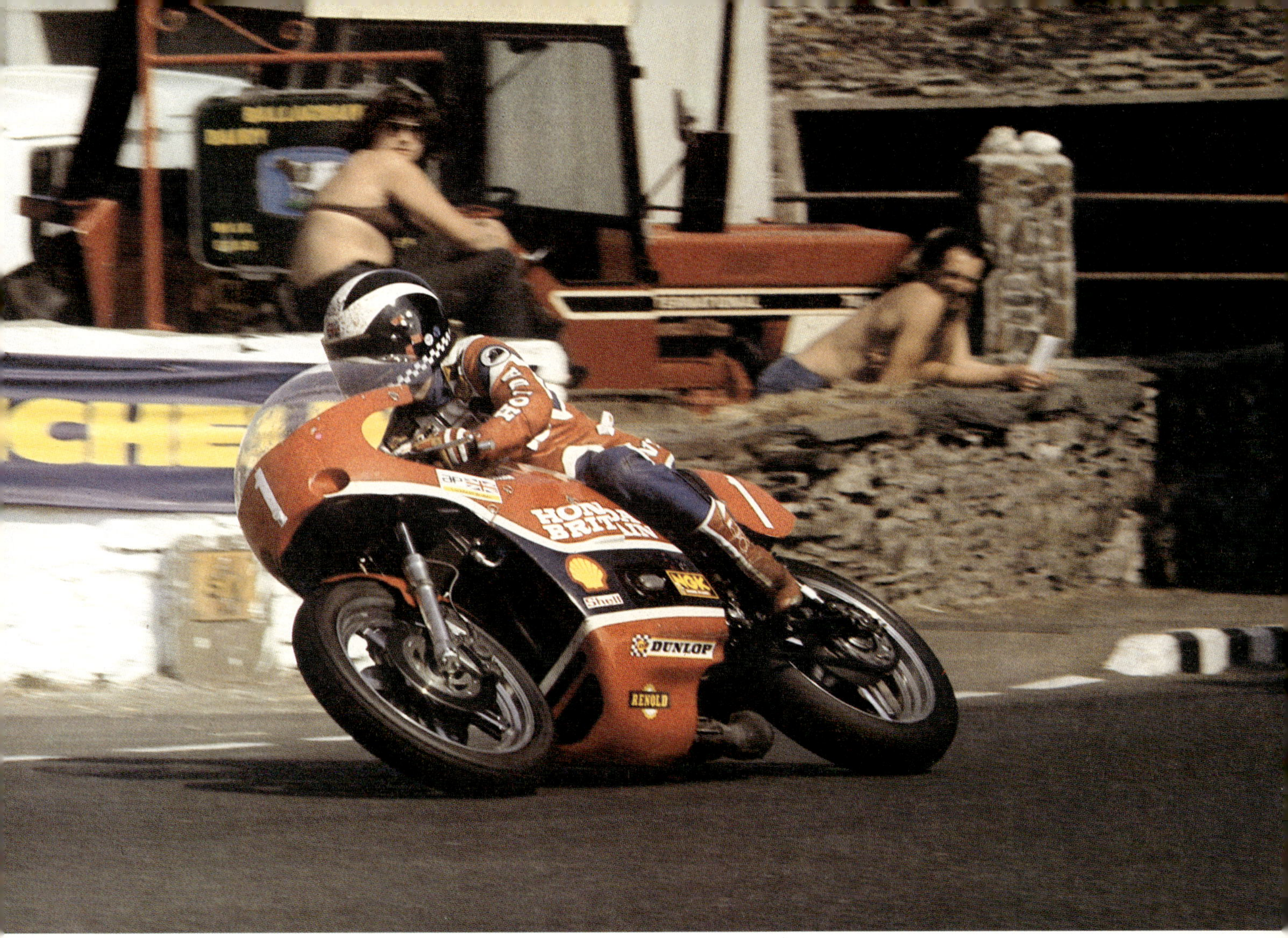
DUNLOP
RENOLD
NOK

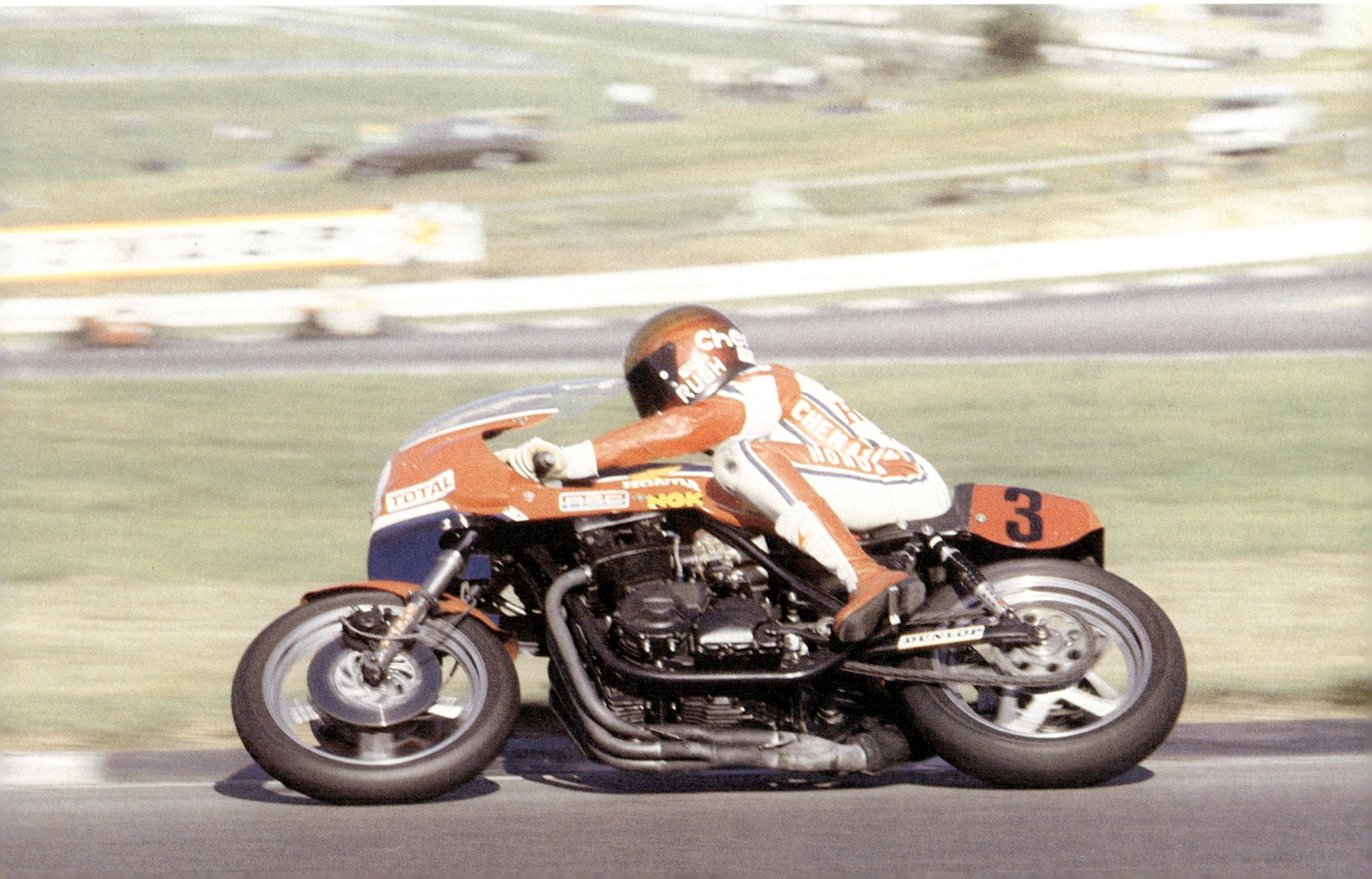
TOTAL
NOK
3
DUNLOP

Christian Leon working flat out at Thruxton to keep his Honda team-mate Stan Woods at bay in the final round of the 1977 Coupe d'Endurance series. Woods partnered by Charlie Williams won the race but Leon and Jean-Claude Chemarin clinched the championship after finishing third

American Steve Baker in the British round of the World 750 cc Championship. Since that day Haslam has brought Honda tremendous success in Britain, winning the TT Formula 1 World Championship and all the major British Championship titles during a five year association which has thrived on mutual respect.

Gerald Davison reflects on that success and remembers he had reservations about Ron when he signed back on that July day in 1977: 'I remember the whole deal cost us £200 plus the use of a van,' he recalled with a smile. 'I must admit that before I met him I thought that Ron was a bit of a tearaway at first but I was completely wrong and he's been with us ever since. After winning that race at Silverstone he's never looked back.'

Haslam led the 12-lap event from start to finish, setting a new lap record in the process, and with the subsequent announcement of a Formula 1 championship series in 1978 the future looked bright for this class.

In Europe the only problem confronting Honda in the Coupe d'Endurance series was whether the title went to Honda France or Honda UK. At the finish of the six-round championship it was the French pair of Leon and Chemarin who clinched the title by just two points from Woods and Williams. A typical example of Honda France's efforts came at the Bol D'Or race when in a 20 minute pit stop they managed to repair a broken frame, sustained when Leon crashed, to win the race by 13 laps.

The whole outcome of the championship rested on the last round at Thruxton deep in Hampshire's rolling chalk downs. Woods and Williams won the race but Leon and Chemarin took the title by finishing third. With Honda machines filling nine of the top ten places in the championship their domination of the series was complete.

Back in Britain the 125 cc championship got off to a cracking start. So close was the championship that no less than eight riders could have

clinched the crown with two rounds remaining. At the finish it was Clive Horton from Derby who earned the £2,300 prize with a first and second in those final rounds. The new series was firmly established as a major attraction at British international meetings.

With so much success in Europe and in Britain it was inevitable that Honda would pitch their considerable expertise and vast financial resources back into the blue riband class of the sport: 500 cc grand prix racing where Yamaha and Suzuki had been making merry for far too many years.

Just two days after Honda UK announced they had signed Phil Read to compete in the Brut Superbike Championship and new Formula 1 series in 1978, the news that everybody had been waiting for broke in Tokyo. At a press conference company president Kawashima revealed that Honda would be returning to the grand prix fray in 1979. He announced they were planning to field a three-man team in the 500 cc class riding four-stroke machinery. The NR500 saga had started.

Back in Britain Honda UK were building Read a special superbike to compete against the all-conquering two-strokes in the Superbike Championship. The motor was based on the endurance-winning unit with a 16-valve cylinder head and double overhead camshafts. They also continued their endurance racing efforts with Woods and Charlie Williams, adding Isle of Man expert John Williams for the TT. But even the best laid plans sometimes go wrong, and at the end of the season the team were disappointed with the results.

Long before the end of the year the relationship with Read became strained and their former grand prix star, the immortal Mike Hailwood, stole all their glory at the TT with his magnificent comeback. Their challenge in the Superbike series never materialised and Haslam had to settle for second spot in the New Formula 1 series.

It was left once again to the endurance men to restore lost pride and Leon and Chemarin duly came up with the goods for the third year in succession, riding a new machine which incorporated a dry clutch and was reported to produce over 130 bhp.

Haslam and Read gave the British team a great boost at the beginning of the year by finishing first and second respectively in the Formula 1 supporting race at the World 750 cc Championship round at Brands Hatch.

However, just a week before the TT Haslam had to settle for third place at Brands Hatch behind the Mocheck-prepared Hondas of Stan Woods and Tony Rutter with Read retiring with engine problems. Just five days later Honda and Read's World TT Formula 1 crown was stolen by Hailwood in a race more suited to the pages of the *Boys Own* comic.

After an 11 year absence the former world champion returned to the Island to win the Formula 1 race and World Championship riding a 864 cc Ducati. He started 50 seconds behind Read but by the third lap had caught him. Read regained his lead on the road after a pit stop but he had pushed the Honda to the limit trying to reduce Hailwood's lead and the engine cried enough. He retired at the 11th milestone. John Williams kept the Honda flag flying by finishing second but the day belonged to Hailwood.

Despite suffering problems Read rode bravely in the Classic, finishing fourth on the 997 cc superbike after six demanding laps. Alan Jackson repeated his triumph in the Formula 2 event with Bill Smith making it a Honda double by clinching the Formula 3 event. A couple of days later, at the tight Mallory Park circuit, Hailwood inflicted another defeat on Read in the Formula 1 championship race. The news was also bleak across the channel where the endurance team lost their first race for two years when mechanical problems and crashes put paid to their chances in the Liège 24-hour race.

Just a week later they bounced back when Leon and Chemarin won the Misano race in Italy

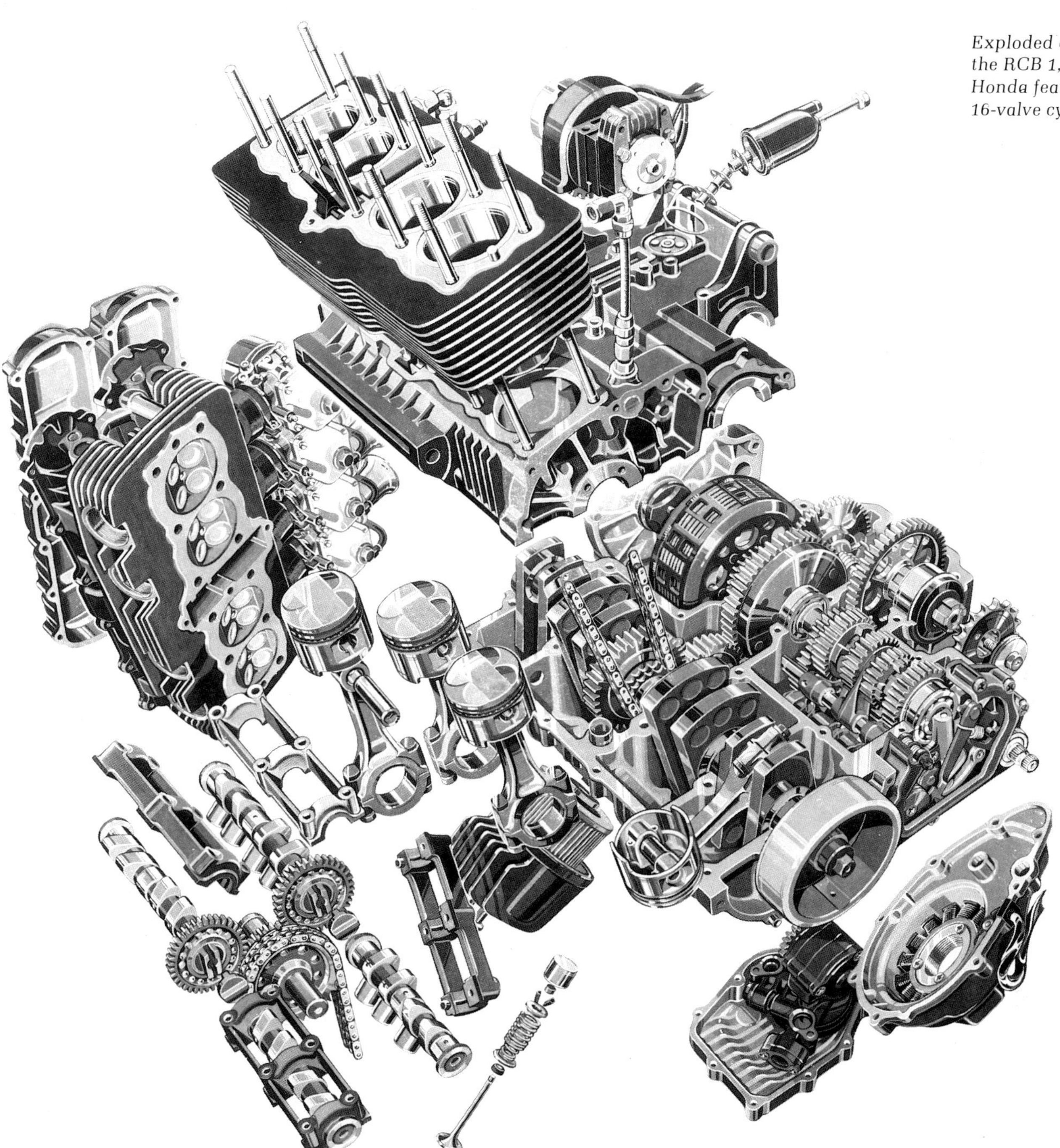

Exploded drawing of the RCB 1,000 cc Honda featuring a 16-valve cylinder head

ahead of Williams and Gary Green, riding in place of the injured Woods. Leon and Chemarin repeated the dose seven days later in the 8-hour race at the notorious German Nürburgring with Williams and Green second again. So despite the opening hiccup Honda were once again ruling the endurance roost.

At this time, it was rumoured in Britain that Honda and Read were about to split up, fuelled when Read did not ride in the Formula 1 championship round at Donington. Matters were not helped with Haslam having to settle for second place behind Roger Marshall riding a Mocheck Honda in that race. The break-up seemed inevitable when Read failed to ride at Silverstone and Ulster, taking a holiday in Spain instead. The official Honda UK team's embarrassment was complete when Tom Herron and Tony Rutter, riding the privately-entered Mocheck Honda machines, filled the first two places in Ulster.

Less than a week later Honda and Read announced they had gone their separate ways. However, despite the differences of opinion at the finish, the former world champion had done much to put Honda back on the racing map.

On the endurance front it was the same old story with Leon and Chemarin making it a Honda hat-trick at the Bol D'Or, clinching the title by finishing second in the final round at Brands Hatch. A month later, at the same venue, Haslam brought some joy to the British camp by winning the final round of the Formula 1 championship with Read, now riding a Mocheck Honda, third. The Brands meeting also produced a fairy tale for Rod Scivyer when he clinched the Honda 125 cc championship 12 years after winning the British 125 cc title on a Honda CR92 four-stroke!

Away from the racing, the Research and

Opposite, top: *spectacular action as Australian Wayne Gardner of the Honda Great Britain race team wheelies his way to a win at Cadwell Park in 1982*

Opposite, bottom: *the very compact layout of the 1982 Honda V-four 1,024 cc racer is well illustrated in this shot of Mike Baldwin as he forces on to fourth place in the Daytona 200*

Classic shot of a classic champion with Jean-Claude Chemarin in action through the trees at Barcelona's famous Montjuich Park in 1979 on his way to yet another Coupe d'Endurance crown

Development Department in Japan were working flat out on the machine that was going to spearhead their return to grand prix racing. They admitted in September that their plans were falling behind schedule and that the grand prix debut of their new machine would not be until halfway through the 1979 season. At the end of the year they signed the experienced Mick Grant from Kawasaki to ride and test the grand prix four-stroke and to compete in Britain in the new Forward Trust/*Motor Cycle Weekly* Formula 1 Championship and the TT.

A year of great triumphs and contrasting disappointments would be the best way to describe Honda's fortunes in 1979. The grand prix debut of the controversial NR500 was a disaster and doubts were already being cast about the ability of a four-stroke engine to match the two-strokes in world championship racing. However, at home Scotsman Alex George and that former 'tearaway' Ron Haslam gave them a clean sweep in the TT and Formula 1 championships which did much to dismiss the NR500 blues.

With pressure building on them from the start of the season Honda gave the NR500 its debut at the British Grand Prix at Silverstone long before they were ready. Amidst the glare of publicity from the world's press the machines ridden by Mick Grant and Japanese former world 350 cc champion Takazumi Katayama sounded beautiful but were painfully slow. Katayama just qualified and Grant got in as a reserve for the race that heralded Honda's return to grand prix racing after a 12 year absence.

If the Honda performance in practice was bad the race was a disaster, with Grant crashing on the first lap and the bike catching fire and Katayama retiring early on. Worse was to follow at the next grand prix in France when both machines failed to qualify but were wheeled onto the grid as reserves. Instead of being wheeled away when it was obvious nobody was going to drop out they stayed and amidst great confusion track officials had to intervene and the bikes were eventually wheeled off the circuit unraced.

It was tough Scotsman, Alex George, who did much to restore Honda's pride with a magnificent double at the TT which even overshadowed the performance of the one and only 'Mike the Bike' on his last TT appearance. George only got the works Formula 1 997 cc Honda because Mick Grant was suffering from an injury but he certainly made the most of his good fortune by comfortably winning the race, beating Charlie Williams riding a Maxton-framed Honda by nearly two minutes with Ron Haslam third on

The saga begins with former 350 cc world champion Takazumi Katayama giving the NR500 four-stroke its first outing at the 1979 British Grand Prix at Silverstone

the second machine of the works team.

George's greatest triumph came five days later in the Classic when on his own admission he was sad to beat Hailwood riding the works 500 cc Suzuki in a race that lived up to its Classic billing. At the finish he beat the maestro by just 3.4 seconds, riding the Formula 1 machine that Haslam piloted to third place earlier in the week. George led by 9.2 seconds at the end of the first lap but Hailwood closed the gap to 4 seconds by the end of the second. By the fifth lap Hailwood led by a mere four-fifths of a second but by Ramsey on the last lap George had fought back to lead and he held onto the slenderest of margins to win a famous victory in one of the greatest races held over the famous 36.75-mile (58.8-km) Mountain circuit.

Alan Jackson completed Honda's joy by winning the Formula 2 race once again, and for the first time the TT Formula world championships included the Ulster Grand Prix in August as a second and final round of the championships. Haslam comfortably won the Formula 1 race, breaking the lap record in the process, to clinch the world championship crown while Jackson followed suit in the Formula 2 event to make it a hat-trick of world championship successes.

Haslam completed a notable double by winning the Forward Trust/*Motor Cycle Weekly* Championship despite a spirited challenge by a newcomer from New Zealand, Graeme Crosby riding a Moriwaki Kawasaki.

From that moment on Crosby was to become a constant thorn in Honda's side, especially when he signed for Suzuki at the beginning of the 1980 season.

Grant finished third in the championship, fighting off the disappointments and frustrations of the NR500 and injuries, with George sharing fourth place.

With so much time and effort being spent trying to make the NR500 competitive Honda's efforts in the FIM Coupe d'Endurance took a bit of a back seat with only one official works machine, ridden by the champions Leon and Chemarin, being entered through Honda France. For the 24-hour races one RCB machine was also made available under French Japauto colours. Despite their lack of official team-mates Leon and Chemarin regained their championship crown but only after a tough battle from a new source – the French Kawasaki duo of Christian Huguet and Herve Moineau.

The two French-based teams fought a fascinating duel with the previously all-conquering

Honda pair coming out on top, both in the championship and the vitally important French Bol D'Or race. With the championship gaining world status the following year there were plenty of challengers to Honda's superiority lining up.

Unhappily it became very apparent during 1980 that Honda had made an expensive mistake by pinning their faith in a four-stroke machine to recapture their grand prix glory. Despite some hard riding by both Takazumi and Mick Grant it was painfully obvious that the NR500, despite all its technical innovations, was neither fast nor reliable enough to mount any sort of challenge against the dominant two-strokes.

Despite a new Ron Williams tubular frame and completely revised engine the new bike did not make an appearance until August. Then, in Finland, Katayama qualified last but failed to make the race blowing up both engines in practice. At the British Grand Prix at Silverstone Katayama rode like a demon to finish fifteenth at the ultra fast circuit. One year after its debut the NR500 had improved but not enough to be competitive. Katayama ended the season with another fine ride, finishing twelfth around the demanding Nürburgring circuit in Germany at the final grand prix. Already the idea of swallowing their pride and building a two-stroke engine was being formulated in Japan.

Away from the gloom of the grands prix the endurance team fought off a considerable Suzuki challenge in the seven-round world series although it produced two new champions in Marc Fontan and Herve Moineau. Honda's new boys Fontan and Moineau won the opening round at Assen in Holland with reigning champions Leon and Chemarin second. The champions redressed the balance at the second round at the German Nürburgring after Fontan crashed in the early stages.

Suzuki scored their first ever endurance win in the next round at Zeltweg in Austria with the Kawasaki pair of Christian Huguet and Richard Hubin second. The Suzuki pair of Jean-Bernard Peyre and Pierre-Etienne Samin lead the championship after finishing fourth as Suzuka in Japan but Fontan and Moineau regained their lead by winning the penultimate round at the Liège 24-hours race at Spa in Belgium and took the championship by finishing second in the last round at Misano in Italy. The British pairing of Haslam and Marshall briefly led the Suzuka race riding a new machine featuring monoshock suspension, but a rear tyre change and a broken chain relegated them to sixth place.

In Britain Honda fought a gloves-off duel with Suzuki, both in the TT world and FT/MCW Formula 1 Championships which produced magnificent racing, a few harsh words and plenty of controversy. Despite his grand prix disappointments evergreen Mick Grant spearheaded their efforts at the TT, the first round of the TT Formula 1 World Championship; the previous year's hero Alex George was eliminated by a crash in practice.

Grant scored his first Honda-mounted TT win in the Formula 1 race which produced quite a lot of controversy. The trouble began even before the race started when Honda objected to Suzuki moving their rider Graeme Crosby from number 3 to 11 on the start line to share the same start time as Grant. But the real aggro came after the race which Grant won from Crosby with Sam McClements (Honda) third and Alan Jackson (Moriwaki-Kawasaki) fourth. The thirsty Honda had completed the race with only one pit stop and Gordon Pantall, entrant of fourth finisher Alan Jackson who had to stop twice, protested that the Honda's tank carried more fuel than the permitted 24 litres. A special meeting of the international jury threw out the protest though Grant admitted that he had ridden with a 28-litre tank but only used 24 litres of fuel, filling the unused space with ping pong balls!

However, it was at the second round of the championship, the Ulster Grand Prix, that team tactics really took over with Suzuki pinching Honda's crown. They signed Ulster favourite Joey Dunlop to help Crosby and he did just that. Dunlop built up a massive lead but then, acting under orders, he let Haslam and Crosby through which meant Grant in fourth place had to displace Dunlop from third place to win the championship. When Haslam slipped off on the last lap it was all over with Crosby winning the race and the championship and Dunlop second. At the end of the season Honda made sure such tactics did not happen again when they signed Dunlop for the 1981 season from right under Suzuki's noses.

Haslam brought some joy to the Honda camp by winning the Formula 3 race on his 390 cc four-stroke machine which clinched the world crown but he was not having so much luck defending his Forward Trust/*Motor Cycle Weekly* championship crown which was again a straight fight between the might of Honda and Suzuki.

At the finish it was veteran Mick Grant who kept the title for Honda but it so nearly went Suzuki's way with Graeme Crosby almost snatching the title after a late start. Again tactics played a considerable part especially when Grant clinched the title at the penultimate round at Cadwell Park. On the last lap of the race Haslam let Grant into third place which clinched the championship for the Yorkshireman, avoiding a nail-biting confrontation with Suzuki at the final round. Although Honda had clinched the title their domination of British Formula 1 racing was coming under tremendous fire from Suzuki with Crosby's winning performances in the last five rounds of the championship a warning of the battles that lay ahead in 1981. Despite winning the title Grant was not re-signed for those battles. Instead TT lap record holder Dunlop was brought in to replace him.

A new name appeared on the Honda 125 championship trophy with Yorkshireman Phil Mellor winning the title after another hard fought series which was only decided at the last round.

Across the Atlantic Honda officially joined the fray for the first time, entering a four-man team consisting of Freddie Spencer, Ron Pierce, Steve

A sunny day at Spa as American Freddie Spencer heads for victory in the 500 cc class of the 1982 Belgian Grand Prix on the two-stroke NS500. It was Honda's first road racing world championship win for 15 years

Arai
BATES
23

FORD
HONDA

Honda rule at the opening grand prix of the 1983 season in South Africa with no less than four NS500s, ridden by Takazumi Katayama, Freddie Spencer, Marco Lucchinelli and Ron Haslam leading on the first lap. Spencer went on to win with Haslam third

Above: Freddie Spencer and the NS500 – a combination that most experts feel will bring Honda their first world 500 cc crown

Opposite, top: *making a good start to the 1983 season Freddie Spencer cranks his NS500 around a right-hander during his winning ride in the South African Grand Prix*

Opposite, bottom: *maximum acceleration! Ron Haslam guns his factory NS500 racer out of a corner during the 1983 Italian Grand Prix*

McLaughlin and Mike Baldwin in the Superbike Championship. The series turned into a three-cornered battle between Spencer, Wes Cooley and Eddie Lawson and the might of Honda, Suzuki and Kawasaki. At the finish of the controversial championship in which everybody seemed to be bending the rules, Spencer, riding the 1,025 cc Honda was third, after winning three races, behind Lawson (Kawasaki) and Cooley (Suzuki). But for the first time his name was in the headlines, and a year later Honda were pinning their grand prix hopes on his slim but very capable shoulders.

Looking back Honda will point to 1981 as the year of transition that saw them building a two-stroke grand prix machine, signing a world champion to ride it, losing their domination of the World Endurance championship and battling hard in Britain.

With Katayama (and briefly Freddie Spencer at Silverstone) finding world championship points an impossibility on the NR500, rumours circulated all year that Honda were building a two-stroke. And just before Christmas they unveiled their first ever two-stroke grand prix road racing machine, the NS500. Two months earlier they had lured Italian world 500 cc champion Marco Lucchinelli away from Suzuki to spearhead their new grand prix team on the new V3 machines. Spencer joined him, giving up his American commitments for his first full season of grand prix racing, with Katayama completing a formidable trio. The transition was complete although Honda promised that NR500 was not buried for good and would be seen later in the year with Haslam getting the chance of a ride.

Their grand prix disappointments were compounded by the dejection suffered on the endurance scene where for the first time for six years Honda machinery did not win the coveted title. The all-conquering team of Leon and Chemarin broke up. Tragically Leon was killed testing a Suzuki in Japan while Chemarin defected to Kawasaki. Honda pinned their hopes on the American duo of Mike Baldwin and Dave Aldana backed up by the French pair, Dominique Sarron and Jean-Claude Jaubert. Sadly neither pair could match the expertise of Leon and Chemarin while the machines could not equal the reliability of the Kawasaki of new champions Raymond Roche and Jean Lafond. Neither of the two Kawasaki works machines failed to finish a race chalking up four wins, two seconds and two thirds.

Back in Britain the picture was also grim on the Formula 1 front which, like its endurance counterpart, had long been in Honda's firm grip.

A naked NS500 with its new frame as it appeared after the 1982 mid-season

Their attack on Crosby's World TT Formula crown at the Isle of Man sparked off the biggest controversy ever seen on the Island. Suzuki-mounted Crosby was delayed by 45 seconds at the start of the race replacing a rear wheel sprocket. Because he missed his starting slot he was not allowed to set off until all riders had started. An announcement stated that he would not be credited with the six minutes he had lost, effectively ruling him out.

Honda later claimed that, as their men Dunlop and Haslam had been kept in touch with proceedings, they had slowed them when Suzuki challenger Grant retired on the second lap with a bent valve. Crosby rode a superb race, setting a new Formula 1 lap record, but at the finish Haslam was garlanded the winner with Dunlop second and Crosby third. It was only when poor 'Rocket Ron' was on his way to a victory celebration that he learnt that Suzuki had protested and that the International Jury had decided that the ACU were wrong in docking Crosby the six minutes. With the time adjusted Crosby was the winner.

Honda were so dismayed by the decision they threatened to leave the Island for good, but happily for the TT they stayed. They registered their protest by dressing their riders in all black leathers to ride all black machinery in the Classic race. It was a ploy that misfired when Dunlop's progress was halted when he ran out of petrol half a mile from his pit and had to push in before restarting. This wrecked his big challenge to Crosby's lead. Dunlop's only consolation was to set a new absolute lap record on his 1,123 cc Honda but when Haslam retired on the third lap Honda's cup of woe was overflowing.

At the second and final round of the championship in Ulster, Haslam was simply unbeatable on the wet 7.4-mile (11.9-km) public roads of the Dundrod circuit. Crosby finished second and the pair tied with 27 points apiece at the top of the table, but the Suzuki man took the title by having a better overall time for the two races.

He repeated the dose in the FT/MCW F1 championship with an impressive display which earned him the sack from Suzuki! Crosby then nearly joined Honda America for 1982 before signing up to ride works Yamahas in Giacomo Agostini's grand prix team. Young Australian Wayne Gardner arrived in Britain, riding a Moriwaki-Kawasaki in similar style to Crosby a couple of years earlier, and Honda were so impressed with his performance they signed him for 1982.

Haslam made up for his Formula 1 disappointments by giving Honda their first success in the Superbike championship. Riding the 1,123 cc Williams-framed four-stroke superbike, he fought off a bevy of two-stroke challenges and Gardner on the four-stroke Kawasaki. Twice, while riding a Yamaha, the 24-year-old Midlander had been pipped at the final round of the championship but this time he made no such mistakes, finishing third in the double-points scoring round at Brands Hatch. Sadly his success was tempered by the tragic death of 1979 and 1980 winner Dave Potter.

Typically Haslam did not forget him when celebrating his victory. 'I've been trying for years to win this title and I'm delighted. But without Dave Potter it just does not feel like the same,' he said.

The Langley Mill man gave himself and Honda a welcome double by completely dominating the new Streetbike series on his standard CB1100R machine. He won the first seven rounds, missing out at the eighth when he crashed, although he remounted to finish second.

The combination of Mellor and his Granby Motors Honda proved the winning combination in the Honda 125 cc Championship once again but sadly it was revealed that the championship had been run for the last time.

'When we started the championship five years ago it revitalised 125 cc racing but that class has now become the domain of the specialist,' explained Gerald Davison.

In America, Spencer, who had turned down a massive Yamaha grand prix offer to ride one more year at home for Honda, finished second in the Superbike championship and third in the Formula 1 before packing his bags for Europe.

In fact 'Fast Freddie's' first race for the Honda grand prix team was in the only non-European grand prix of the year – the Argentine event that started the 1982 season. And in a race seen on television by millions all around the world he fought out a tremendous high speed battle with Yamaha aces Kenny Roberts and Barry Sheene. Roberts won from Sheene but, with Spencer a close third and Lucchinelli and Katayama in the first six, Honda proved that their new two-stroke challenge had to be taken very seriously indeed. Spencer continued to star throughout the season, chalking up Honda's first grand prix win for 15 years in Belgium and winning again in the San Marino Grand Prix run in Italy. Spencer was also victorious in the first three grands prix of 1983 – the South African at Kyalami, the French race at Le Mans and the Italian GP at Monza. The relatively simple three-cylinder NS500 two-stroke had proved to be as promising as the NR500 had been disappointing and a new era of Honda participation in road racing had begun.

Bikes the World Never Saw

The brand new motor cycle that glistens on the showroom floor may be the answer to someone's dreams but its design and manufacture take much longer than most people expect. Honda spends a large proportion of its budget on research and development, and this finances projects which may, or may not, reach the production stage.

There is a fair chance that Honda has produced a motor cycle in most of the configurations possible (especially with engines), either as a prototype, and have proceeded with it or discarded it, or they are about to do so. One example is the six-cylinder Gold Wing. There were many rumours of a larger version of the famous flat-four, with artists impressions appearing in many papers, but in fact the machine had already been made. Code-named the AOK, the flat-six preceded the flat-four and was the beginning of the development project that led to both the six-cylinder CBX1000 and the four-cylinder GL1000 Gold Wing. The original idea was for a 'King of Kings' motor cycle and in 1972 development was started. The brief was for a grand touring motor cycle that should be superior to the competition in both smoothness and performance. Furthermore, the machine should have character and class.

When Honda realised that a machine with a super sports and grand touring theme could not be combined into one model, they divided the development programme. The CBX, with a six-cylinder, air-cooled, in-line across-the-frame engine, became the super sports flagship. It had a top speed of 140 mph (225 kph) and a quarter-mile time of 11.75 seconds. This made it one of the

With the rear end straight from BMW and a very similar front end to that which was eventually used on the four-cylinder Gold Wing, this six-cylinder prototype code-named AOK is a real 'bitsa'

fastest machines of its day, thanks to the double overhead camshafts and the six 28 mm carburettors. The engine churned out 105 bhp at 9,000 rpm and the bike weighed in at 558 lb (253 kg). But the CBX did not actually materialise until 1978. In 1972 it still seemed possible that one machine could be both the super sports and the grand touring supremo. The AOK had a total capacity of 1,470 cc. It would have been the largest capacity, mass production roadster but it was developed to a relatively mild state of tune to produce only 80 bhp at a leisurely 6,700 rpm. It weighed about 500 lb (227 kg) and reached a top speed of 130 mph (209 kph) so was obviously a better touring machine than a sportster.

When Honda discovered that they could get equal performance from less capacity, they discarded two of the six cylinders. Retaining almost the same bore and stroke at 72 mm and 61.4 mm, the Gold Wing had a capacity of 1,000 cc. The maximum power of the 1975 model was 80 bhp at 7,500 rpm. They retained the performance of the six on the four-cylinder by increasing the compression ratio and the number of carburettors. The finished machine weighed 616 lb (280 kg) so either it had gained a lot of fat since it was a six-cylinder prototype or the development department claim of 500 lb (227 kg) for their machine was rather optimistic. The finished article was capable of over 125 mph (200 kph) and a 13 second quarter-mile thanks to the 9.2:1 compression ratio and the four 32 mm Keihin CV carburettors.

The AOK prototype had a lowly 8:1 compression ratio and a double-barrel carburettor, one venturi having a 29 mm bore and the other a 27 mm. These fed into a cast inlet manifold as is common car practice. Another car component was the distributor which was mounted on the left-hand side of the engine. The single-plate dry clutch was another sign of car technology.

When the Gold Wing appeared in public it had lost the single-plate dry clutch in favour of a wet multiplate type more usual for a motor cycle. It had also discarded the distributor in favour of electronic ignition with a vacuum advance and retard mechanism. The four-speed gearbox of the prototype had been replaced by a five-speed box. The intense development programme proved worthwhile because the water-cooled four, first as the GL1000 and then the GL1100, had a long life and attracted a large following of dedicated owner/enthusiasts who were smitten by its effortless performance and reliability.

Although the Gold Wing was the first water-cooled machine produced by Honda, the demand for quiet and efficient engines meant that liquid cooling was to become more common. The next water-cooled engine was to be the CX500 V-twin and its exciting turbocharged brother.

It has been a point of some argument in the press as to how the CX500 Turbo came about. Was the CX500 always designed to be turbocharged or did it gain its forced induction because of impending competition from Yamaha, Suzuki and Kawasaki?

The answer is that in 1975 work was carried out on three projects which together resulted in the production of the CX500 and the CX500 Turbo. The A3S and the A3S II were water-cooled, 80 degree V-twins. They were both 358 cc, and the II was supercharged. The non-

Code-named A3S 11, the CX360 V-twin was the forerunner of the five-hundred. The wheels fitted to this machine were pressed in two halves. The production Comstar wheels are composites, pressed spokes, with separate rims and hubs

With frame tubes running direct from the steering head to the swinging arm pivot and the engine slung underneath, the A3V prototype never saw production but it contributed to Honda's knowledge of forced induction engines

supercharged version was part of a programme to develop a basic bike for the 1980s. Six requisites were laid out for the Japanese designers to consider:

1) It should 'take your breath away' when being driven.
2) It should be comfortable and manoeuvrable.
3) It should make the rider look good.
4) It should be safe to ride and not be tiring.
5) New technology should be applied to make 1 to 4 possible.
6) It should be purchaseable for under $1,000.

Although the criteria may have lost something in their translation from Japanese, the idea is there. The water-cooled V-twin was chosen to be compact and quiet, providing smooth running with the supercharger logically positioned between the two cylinders. The engine design was special in that the cylinder and crankcase were integral.

The non-supercharged engine had a bore and stroke of 72 mm by 44 mm, and was fed by two CV carburettors. The engine had a compression ratio of 10.7:1 but it only produced 38.3 bhp at 10,000 rpm. It was considered that this machine did not meet market requirements in terms of all-round performance. The necessary weight of the water-cooling with the radiator made the machine tip the scales at 332 lb (151 kg) dry, according to the Research and Development (R and D) Department.

It was that the A3S could benefit from increased performance and therefore the capacity was increased to 500 cc with a bore and stroke of 78 mm by 52 mm. The water-cooling and shaft-drive were retained but in some ways the CX500 was a retrograde step. It lost some of the advanced features of the CX360. In the prototype stage Honda had experimented with a single rear suspension unit working off a triangulated, single-sided swing arm, inboard rear disc and leading-axle front suspension.

The wheels that appeared on the CX360 and some other prototypes of the period were never in fact seen in production. They appear to have been made from two pressings, welded and bolted together. There were some production engineering problems and the wheels that eventually arrived in the showrooms were the composite items called 'Comstars'. These have pressed-steel spokes riveted to the extruded aluminium rim. It is a pity as the three-spoked, prototype wheels looked very smart and functional, even better than the five-spoked production items.

The supercharged CX360 was somewhat disappointing in that it only gained 5 hp, although it produced 43 bhp at only 8,500 rpm compared with the 10,000 rpm of a normally-aspirated engine. The compression ratio was taken down to 8.7:1 but the machine weighed another 22 lb (10 kg). The induction was forced by a single-screw compressor, driven off the crankshaft which drew through a single CV carburettor. The

The A3V 360 cc machine looked sporty with its exhaust pipes tucked well in underneath the engine. The third cylinder, used to force gases into the combustion chambers of the driving cylinders, is hidden behind and between the conventional pair

knowledge gained with this supercharger was valuable when it came to making decisions about turbocharging the CX500.

Another group of engines was developed at the same time as the V-twins and these were also intended as prototyes for the basic motor cycle of the 1980s. One became that sturdy workhorse, the CB400T but the more exciting supercharged version never appeared. The normally-aspirated engine was aimed at consolidating Honda's stranglehold on their biggest market. They sold more 350 cc machines in the United States than any other capacity group and America was still the boom market. One of the machines that the twin was intended to replace was the 400 four which, although popular in Europe, had never been a big hit in America. The twin had to have performance and Honda went for an over square engine: a 70 mm bore and a very short, 46.7 mm stroke. It allowed them plenty of valve area and the engine revved freely to 9,500 rpm where it produced 38.5 bhp.

To provide the smoothness equal to the four, the twin had a balancer shaft. Its racy intentions were accentuated by the frame which had the steering head connected directly to the swinging arm pivot. The frame was never seen in production but the engine was hung underneath with two tubes passing either side of the carburettor. It had a five-speed gearbox, chain final drive and disc brakes both front and rear. The floating front caliper was retained on the CB400 but the production model had a drum rear brake. The CB400, with its actual capacity of 395 cc, had a slightly longer stroke of 50.6 mm but a similar bore: 70.5 mm. The compression ratio had been dropped from 9.8:1 to 9.3:1.

The supercharged engine, code-named A3V, had an even lower compression ratio of only 8.5:1. It had a piston compressor running as a third cylinder which also acted as a balancer. The 360 cc twin was fed by 269 cc of compressor cylinder. The combustion cylinders were much less over square with a bore and stroke of 66 mm by 52.6 mm. The compressor cylinder was 74 mm by 62.6 mm. It was fitted between the two cylinders and leaned to the rear. It added another 10 lb (4.5 kg) to the weight of the machine and only 2 hp for a reduction of 500 rpm. The maximum torque though was produced at 4,000 rpm instead of 8,000 rpm on the normally aspirated engine. This gives a clue as to much of the reasoning behind Honda's interest in forced induction. It also helps to explain why the CX500 Turbo was not the all-conquering fire-breather that many were expecting. Honda were investigating forced induction with a view to improving all-round performance and the spread of power rather than just peak engine output. One of the reasons that Honda dropped the piston compressor that they tried on the CB400-style prototype was that, although it provided good mid-range torque, it proved very inefficient at high rpm.

The development of the V-twin that eventually

became the CX500 goes even further back than the A3S water-cooled prototype. In 1973 there existed an air-cooled 90 degree V-twin which was intended as a forerunner of a commuter bike of the 1980s. The idea was to produce a machine that was 'easy to drive, easy to start, had a comfortable cruising speed, light weight and handling with the woman rider in mind and maintenance free.' That was the directive to the development engineers but the target performance of 80 mph (128 kph) was not reached and the project dropped, at least in that guise. One important part of the prototype that survived was the transmission. It had a torque converter and a two-speed sub-transmission with high and low ranges. This was developed for use on the CB750 and CB400 Hondamatics.

The CB750 Hondamatic appeared first in 1976. It was not truly fully automatic in that it had a foot operated gear lever to select neutral, low and high ratios. But it had no handlebar operated clutch and the torque converter coped with its own change in drive ratio from about 2:1 at stall when the engine was straining against the load of the pump, to almost 1:1 when the turbine speed rose to almost 95 per cent of its drive side.

The torque converter eventually used on the CB750 was the same as fitted to Honda's domestic model N360 car and very similar to the one used in the Civic Automatic. The converter had three elements: the first was a centrifugal, hydraulic pump, driven by the engine, which threw oil at a turbine wheel and in turn drove the gearbox shaft. The pump wheel threw many streams of oil at the many veins of the turbine wheel. After hitting the turbine, the oil was forced by the curved housing back to the centre of the turbine where the third wheel caught the streams of oil and deflected them towards the centre of the pump so that they could be circulated again.

The air-cooled three-fifty obviously eventually became the water-cooled five-hundred and the requirement for minimum maintenance that was originally stipulated for the A23 prototype survived and was achieved so that the CX500 needed only very basic attention. Air-cooled V-twins were made both with shaft and chain final drives. Engine development of the A23 was carried out using CB200 running gear, thus making it much easier and cheaper to produce a complete machine capable of being road tested.

Even more of an existing machine was used in 1974 when Honda wanted to investigate rotary engines. Suzuki were already hard at work on their Wankel, the RE5, which made its debut late in 1974. It was a huge motor cycle, weighing 573 lb (260 kg). It was not very fast, had a single rotor with a displacement of 497 cc. It was a smooth tourer but very complicated and expensive; it never gained public acceptance.

Honda never got as far as making the expensive error of trying to mass-produce their Wankel. They did produce a very elegant prototype by grafting a single rotor onto a CB125. Unlike the Suzuki, the Honda was air-cooled,

The 350 cc V-twin A23 was designed to be a commuter machine. This prototype uses CB200 running gear

although it also needed an oil cooler because Wankel engines always produce a lot of heat. The Suzuki was massive and unlike any other motor cycle engine; the Honda, on the other hand, could have passed for an oddly-shaped piston engine. The rotor casing was mounted on top of the CB125 crankcases and the rotor was connected by chain to the original engine's primary drive.

The single rotor had a one chamber capacity of 124.7 cc and a compression ratio of 8.5:1. It produced 13.5 hp at 8,000 rpm, breathing through a 28 mm Keihin carburettor. The chamber had two spark plugs and 100:1 ratio petrol/oil mixture was necessary to preserve the sealing power of the rotor tip. Rotor tip wear has always been a problem and this made the awkward oil mixture a necessity. Honda gave up the project for, although the Wankel offered high power output and possibilities of low weight, there were difficulties in starting, carburation and noise. No doubt many, if not all, of these things could have been solved in time, but the Honda engineers must have taken a good look at the monstrous lump that Suzuki created with their RE5, compared it with the petite simplicity of their prototype and decided that there was nothing to be gained by developing in that direction.

One problem Honda feared that they could never solve with the Wankel was that of exhaust emissions. In the early 1970s exhaust emissions were becoming a major source of concern, considering impending American regulations. Rotary engines have a poor reputation in that area and even conventional reciprocating engines needed development to improve their combustion performance. Honda were looking ahead to the 1975 Edmund Muskie Act. They had been developing a special engine for use in their automobiles, called the CVCC engine. This referred to the Compound Vortex Controlled Combustion. Whereas most car manufacturers were having to develop heavy and expensive catalytic converters, Honda's car engines survived the 1970s without them, thanks to the CVCC. The principle was to provide the combustion chamber with a stratified charge. Instead of one uniform mixture the incoming charge would be divided into two: a rich charge directed towards the spark plug, surrounded by a weaker charge.

The CVCC car engines had two different-sized inlet valves. The large valve was situated next to the exhaust valve and was fed by an air/fuel mixture at a very lean 20:1. A smaller valve fed a small pre-combustion chamber next to the plug with a rich 7:1 ratio. The overall mixture was something like 16:1, which in a normal combustion chamber could never be ignited, being far too lean. But in the CVCC head the 7:1 ratio was ignited first and the flame spread to the weaker 20:1 mixture. This system was a breakthrough for Honda in the car world but its application in a motor cycle was more difficult. The cylinder head was required to run at high temperature, easy enough to control with a water-cooled engine, but difficult with air-cooling. The head is also bulky and ugly, and it was difficult to adapt to the

The tiny, two-speed gearbox for the automatic transmission can be seen above the left-hand foot-rest. Even though it is air-cooled, this V-twin is obviously from the same family that bred the CX500

engines of the era. This prototype CVCC engine had a bore and stroke of 54 mm by 50.6 mm, producing a capacity of 325 cc with a compression ratio of 8.9:1. Maximum power was only 22.5 hp at 7,500 rpm. This did not compare well with the standard engines of the period.

Honda found it difficult to reconcile the resulting performance with the requirements of the motor cycle market, although the control of exhaust emission was impressive. They achieved the 3.4 g/m carbon monoxide emission required by the 1975 regulations. The engine produced only 0.65 g/m nitrous oxide while the regulations allowed 3.1. It fell down on the hydrocarbon emission, producing 0.9 g/m instead of the allowed 0.41.

By more conventional combustion engine development Honda have reduced their combustion mixtures to 14:1, thus they are approaching the 16:1 achieved by the CVCC engine. The increased use of water-cooling allows them to elevate combustion temperatures and control emissions.

These unique revelations as to some of the machines that have otherwise never been seen outside of Honda's R and D Department give some idea of the tremendous amount of work involved in producing the machines that you can buy. A further measure of the effort involved is that these prototypes preceded the production machines by as much as five years in some cases. That gives an idea of how much more work is involved in refining, styling and 'productionising' the prototypes.

These are the bikes that populated Honda's R and D Department from 1972 to 1976. Since then those hallowed halls have seen several more generations of engines, some of which we shall never see, but some will become the superbikes and commuter transport of the future.

Opposite, top: *that peculiar lump grafted onto the top of a CB125 is a rotary cylinder. This A16 prototype looks simple and reasonably smart*

Opposite, bottom: *the bottom half of the A16 prototype engine is conventional four stroke. A dummy crankshaft takes the drive from the rotary crank via a chain on the right-hand side of the engine. The rev counter drive can be seen on the end of the rotary crank*

Above and right: *this A11 prototype CVCC (Compound Vortex Controlled Combustion) has a large, complicated carburettor and a huge lump of an exhaust manifold. The diaphragm box for the ignition advance and retard can be seen just protruding up the side of the fuel tank*

Models through the Years

NCZ50 Motocompo Trunkbike (Japanese specification)

ST50M Dax (Japanese specification)

Whatever kind of motor cycling, from schoolboy scrambling to long-distance touring, Honda have a bike designed just for it. And no wonder, for the world's biggest motor cycle manufacturer has the world's biggest range – over 130 models world-wide!

The world is Honda's oyster – they export to countries as diverse as China and Peru and so they must cater for tastes as far apart as, say, a Californian college student and a Nigerian farm worker. But of course it is not only a question of taste. Honda also have to tailor their bikes to meet widely differing national legislation: this means that the popular CX500, for example, must be built as a 400 cc machine for the French market – and the awesome CBX 1000 cc six-cylinder superbike must be detuned slightly to come within the West German 100 bhp maximum power restrictions.

Honda's extensive range runs from the tiny, 118.5 cm-long NCZ50 Motocompo Trunkbike launched at the 1981 Tokyo show, designed with retractable seat and folding handlebars so that it can be stowed in the back of the new Honda City minicar, to the GL1100 Gold Wing Aspencade luxury cruiser launched in the USA, with its own digital stereo radio and CB radio options! In between there are Hondas that transport Australian farmers across vast acreages, Hondas that are replicas of world championship-winning moto cross machines and shatteringly fast street Hondas that offer experienced riders the ultimate riding experience.

Honda's philosophy is to try and cater for all tastes ... They want to please all of the people all of the time! As an official Honda statement explains: 'There are Hondas for people from all walks of life: models for sport, models for amusement, business ... everything. Every age group, from youngsters to housewives, have their transport needs met perfectly by Honda.'

Because the 50 cc to 125 cc market is the biggest world-wide, Honda provide more choice in this capacity class than in any other. The range is vast: over 20 50 cc models alone in varying sizes and styles, and with both two- and four-stroke engines.

Apart from the little Motocompo foldaway

machine mentioned earlier Honda offer several different true mini-bikes. There are the intriguing little Z50J Monkey and Gorilla fun bikes that both use a derivative of the 50 cc four-stroke ohc semi-automatic motor that is at the heart of the hugely successful C50, 70 and 90 range of step-through scooterettes. Fun bikes they may be, but they all have proper lighting and meet all the necessary regulations to make them road legal. Sales of both, however, are largely restricted to Japan. Another fun bike is the ST50 Dax that uses basically the same motor but with a four-ratio gear-box.

Without a doubt the most popular Hondas ever are the C50-C90 scooterettes of which over 15 million have been sold throughout the last 25 years. Of course the machines have been refined and updated considerably since the C100 Super Cub was launched in 1958. The latest series of scooterettes based on this design are the C50L and C50L automatic, both restricted performance machines designed to comply with many European 30 mph maximum speed moped restrictions. The former has a three-speed semi-automatic gearbox where the rider selects the ratios while the latter is completely automatic.

The up to date C50, C70 and C90 machines – the C90 is Great Britain's most successful powered two-wheeler – all have the new 'econopower engine' and an automatic clutch. In Japan there is a C75 and in the USA the C70 Passport has the added refinement of electric starting. Closely related to the scooterettes are the CF50 and 70 Chaly step-throughs that use little 10-inch wheels.

Mopeds

Honda's range of restricted performance mopeds is huge; there are stylish mopeds, plain mopeds, mopeds with electric starters, chopper mopeds, and motor cycle-style mopeds.

Apart from the C50L and C50L automatic mentioned earlier, there is the NS50 Melody that has also topped the sales charts in the United Kingdom. Powered by a two-stroke motor, the Melody comes with 12-volt electrics, an automatic gearbox and weather protection; there is even the Melody Deluxe that features electric starting.

At the bottom end of the price table is the bargain-basement PA50 Camino with single-speed gearbox and pedal starting. In between there are the incredibly successful Express mopeds – also known as the Roadpal – which were promoted in the United Kingdom by model-turned-actress Twiggy and the new NX50 scooter-style Caren that has a completely automatic gearbox and up-to-date 12-volt electrics.

For the young, and not so young, riders who want a more sporty moped, there are the recently introduced MB and MT range of up-to-the-minute two-stroke roadsters. The MB50S is a real little road racer with race-developed beam-type frame, disc front brake, Comstar wheels and a high performance two-stroke motor that features a novel balancer shaft design. Japanese riders can pick the chopper-style MB50 Raccoon. There is

C70 Passport (US specification)

NS50 Melody

NX50 Caren (Taiwan specification)

SC50 Squash (Japanese specification)

NV50 Stream (Japanese specification)

also the MT50S trail bike moped that, like its street-based brother, has a five-speed gearbox. A new model is the MTX50 enduro-style machine which has all the latest equipment and Pro Link monoshock rear suspension. Incidentally, in many countries all the above are available in 80 cc versions for those riders who wish to progress in power a little.

For those moped riders who want to have the benefits of four-stroke power when they venture out onto the trail there is the XL50S trail bike with its rugged sohc power unit, high level exhaust, knobbly tyres and 9.5 bhp motor.

Still a moped – in strict definition – is the CB50S that has big bike looks. Very much a no-nonsense machine this bike is still available in several countries though it was dropped from the UK range recently. It has a four-stroke motor, tubular frame, dual seat and front single disc brake.

In Japan there is a neat little scooterette, powered by a two-stroke motor, that runs on tiny little 8-inch wheels and goes under the unlikely name of Squash. Of course this little 128 cm-long machine qualifies as a moped.

The very latest idea in moped design is the new Honda Stream three-wheeler. Although there have been three-wheeler mopeds before, the Honda Stream is really the transport of the 1980s. It has a hinged body that allows the rider to lean the front portion into bends while the rear motor/drive wheels unit remains upright.

Unlike a previous three-wheeler, the Stream has a differential clutch at the rear for unfussy cornering. And the 4 bhp two-stroke motor is capable of a whopping 209 mpg (1.35 litres/100 km). The 8-inch (20.3-cm) tyres and long (121 cm) wheelbase allows unrivalled legroom and comfort; to make riding simple an electric starter is fitted, and of course both clutch and transmission are automatic.

The link system that allows the machine to be leant round corners incorporates a rubber spring that helps bring the mechanism back up to the vertical. Other novel ideas incorporated in the Stream are radial tyres at the rear for better road-holding, an equaliser mechanism for the rear brakes (one on each wheel), full rear suspension, anti-vibration engine mountings, one-touch parking lock that locks the wheels and a front luggage compartment. There is also an automatic choke and fuel cock as well as a bulb failure warning lamp.

One only has to look at the Stream to see that it is totally unlike anything else ... Honda have put their new moped in a category all of its own: 'Threeter' or three-wheeler scooter. They say that it combines the joy of two-wheeler riding with all the comforts of a car ... they must be right!

Lightweights

Mopeds are not powerful enough for every rider/commuter's needs so Honda developed a series of lightweight motor cycles. Here again the choice is mind-boggling. Apart from the massively popular C50, 70 and 90 cc scooterettes mentioned

CD70 (Pakistan specification)

earlier, Honda have a whole range of genuine lightweight motor cycles designed to cater for all tastes and ... pockets.

Right at the bottom end of the market are the CD50 and CD70 motor cycles that are still fantastically popular in countries as far apart as Brazil and Sri Lanka. Using a pressed-steel backbone frame and a variant of the sohc single-cylinder motor at the heart of the scooterettes, these little machines have a four-speed non-automatic gearbox, dual seat and proper front telescopic suspension. (Many European and American riders will remember the S90 sports machine that was so popular in the 1960s with affection and be interested to learn that it is still available in countries as far afield as Iran, Syria and Nicaragua.)

A complete departure for Honda – who for many years adopted a 'four-stroke only' approach to motor cycle production – was the introduction of the H100 two-stroke roadster in 1980. Futuristically styled with a tubular beam-type frame, this little machine uses a bigger version of the two-stroke motor featured on the MB/MT50. This power unit incorporates a number of new ideas: a balancer shaft is fitted to cut down the vibrations, there are anti-backlash gears and a novel oiling system that more accurately matches the oil injection to throttle opening. Stylishly, and conveniently, both the oil filler and petrol filter are grouped together on the petrol tank, as is the neat oil level gauge. The H100 (also known as the MB100 in some countries) comes with a fully-enclosed drive chain and a simple chain guard option.

Honda produce a whole range of 100, 105 and 125 cc single-cylinder four-stroke machines that all offer unrivalled economy – well over 100 mpg (2.8 litres/100 km) is a commonplace attainment for riders of these machines.

The new CT110 is a semi-step-through with a 105 cc engine which is sold in Japan as a go-anywhere machine. It has a pressed-steel frame, single seat, sensible pannier and tyres that will allow a limited amount of off-road use.

Another series of models in this lightweight range are the CBs. The CB100 single has an sohc motor, dual seat, five-speed gearbox and disc front brake, while the sporty CB125S is virtually identical to its 100 cc brother except in engine size.

For the riders who want a little more refinement there is the GL125 that has a front disc brake, carburettor with Honda's TPFC system (basically an accelerator pump) and the latest square-type front headlamp. The whole package produces a healthy 14 bhp at 10,000 rpm.

For the really economy minded there is the CG110 (105 cc) that has push-rod operated overhead valves for cheapness and dependability. Popular in the United Kingdom is the CG125 that is an overgrown CG110 – a push-rod single that meets the new British 12 bhp/125 cc learner regulations.

In several countries Honda have taken the philosophy that 'the customer must have what he

MB100

CT110 (US specification)

GL125 (Malaysian specification)

CG125 Alcool (Brazilian specification)

CM125 Custom

wants' to incredible lengths. Under their 'Mix and Match' scheme buyers of the CG110 and CG125 can choose different petrol tank styles and capacities, tank and sidepanel colours, disc or drum brakes and even a single or dual seat. There are also seven different colour schemes to select from!

An interesting variant on the 125 cc single theme is the revolutationary CG125 Alcool developed jointly by Honda Japan and their Brazilian subsidiary. As its name suggests the Alcool is designed to run on the ethanol-based alcohol fuel that is sold alongside petroleum in Brazilian filling stations. The ethanol, produced from the fermentation of vegetable and sugar products, is a cheap alternative to petrol.

The Alcool 125 has a modified carburettor to cope with the different fuel and other modifications to allow the motor to burn the alcohol-air mixture efficiently. It is not available anywhere else in the world.

In keeping with their policy of giving the customer the maximum possible choice Honda have a range of four 125 cc twins. For the commuter type who wants a simple machine there is the CD125 with deeply valanced mudguards, heel and toe gearchange, and chunky simple good looks. The CD125 is available in Japan with a dual seat or pillion-and-pannier option and is sold in the United Kingdom in 12 bhp form to meet the new learner restrictions.

The CM125T is a 'chopper-style' bike with high handlebars, easy riding position, generously padded dual seat, electric start and fat (3.5 × 16 inch) rear tyre. Like all the CD models it has a front drum brake to save on cost.

For sporty riders there is the popular CB125T with its high-performance sohc engine producing a lusty 15 bhp at 11,000 rpm, Comstar wheels, electric starter, front disc brake and racey looks.

New for the 1980s is the 12 bhp restricted CM125T Super Dream designed with the new British learner regulations in mind. Based upon the CB125T this machine more than makes up for the lack of power in the terms of its sophistication. It has the very latest single-shock Pro Link rear suspension, 12-volt electrics, square quartz-halogen headlamp, electric starter and front disc brake. After the success of their step-throughs in the 1960s Honda really established themselves with the incredibly popular C92 and CB92 Benly 125 cc sports twins ... the new CB125T is designed to follow in the Benly's footsteps.

Moving up the capacity range there is a budget no-frills commuter – the CB200 – that is also available in Japan as the CD195 Road Master with detachable pillion seat. Like the other CD models this has a simple four-speed gearbox operated by a heel and toe rocking level to avoid scuffed toes.

Middleweights

One of the biggest-selling Hondas ever is the four-stroke CB250N Dream. Often at the top of the UK motor cycle sales charts this machine is the successor to the classic C72 and CB72 two-fiftys of

CB125T (Japanese specification)

Above, left: *Spacy 125*

Above: *Lead 125*

the 1960s.

Those machines were fitted with electric starters in 1963 and were streets ahead of the opposition then ... just as their successors are! The CB250N Super Dream for the 1980s has a six-speed gearbox, twin carburettors, a three-valve (two inlet, one exhaust) head and is a more refined machine than the old CB72. The CB250 Dream was one of the first Hondas to benefit from the so-called Eurostyle approach. This derives from the high degree of design input from Honda's European importers who wanted machines styled to suit their markets.

The CB250N is available in two standards of trim – the deluxe version has Comstar wheels picked out in black, but all the versions set new highs in smoothness and sophistication. The custom version – the CM250 – is basically the same machine but with fatter rear tyre, well-padded dual seat, high 'bars and a five-speed gearbox. This version is available in the USA, Japan and elsewhere as the CB250T LA Custom with new-style Comstar wheels and other refinements.

A runaway success from the beginning of the 1980s was the sporty single-cylinder CB250RS. This machine was immediately taken to the hearts of many British riders who had been without a 250 cc four-stroke single for years. Using as a starting point the lusty sohc four-valve motor from the XL250 trail bike Honda produced a powerful (26 bhp at 8,500 rpm) machine and equipped it with 12-volt electrics, five-speed gearbox, FVQ rear dampers for superlative roadholding, a front disc brake and quartz-halogen headlamp. The combination of light weight and free revving performance made the CB250RS a firm favourite. Lately Honda have equipped it with an electric starter and still have managed to keep the weight right down to a respectable 288 lb (131 kg) dry.

Spearheading their challenge into the mid-1980s Honda launched a new range of V-engined, high performance machines. There were V-twins, V3s and V4s, in both two- and four-stroke varieties.

At the bottom of the capacity ladder is the VT250F twin – the fastest four-stroke 250 cc machine around. Tests have shown that this high-revving double overhead camshaft 90 degree water-cooled twin is capable of close on 100 mph (160 kph). Honda claim 35 bhp at

CB250N Super Dream

CM250 Custom

CB250T LA Custom (Japanese specification)

CB250RS

VT250F

MVX250F

CB400N Super Dream

VF400F

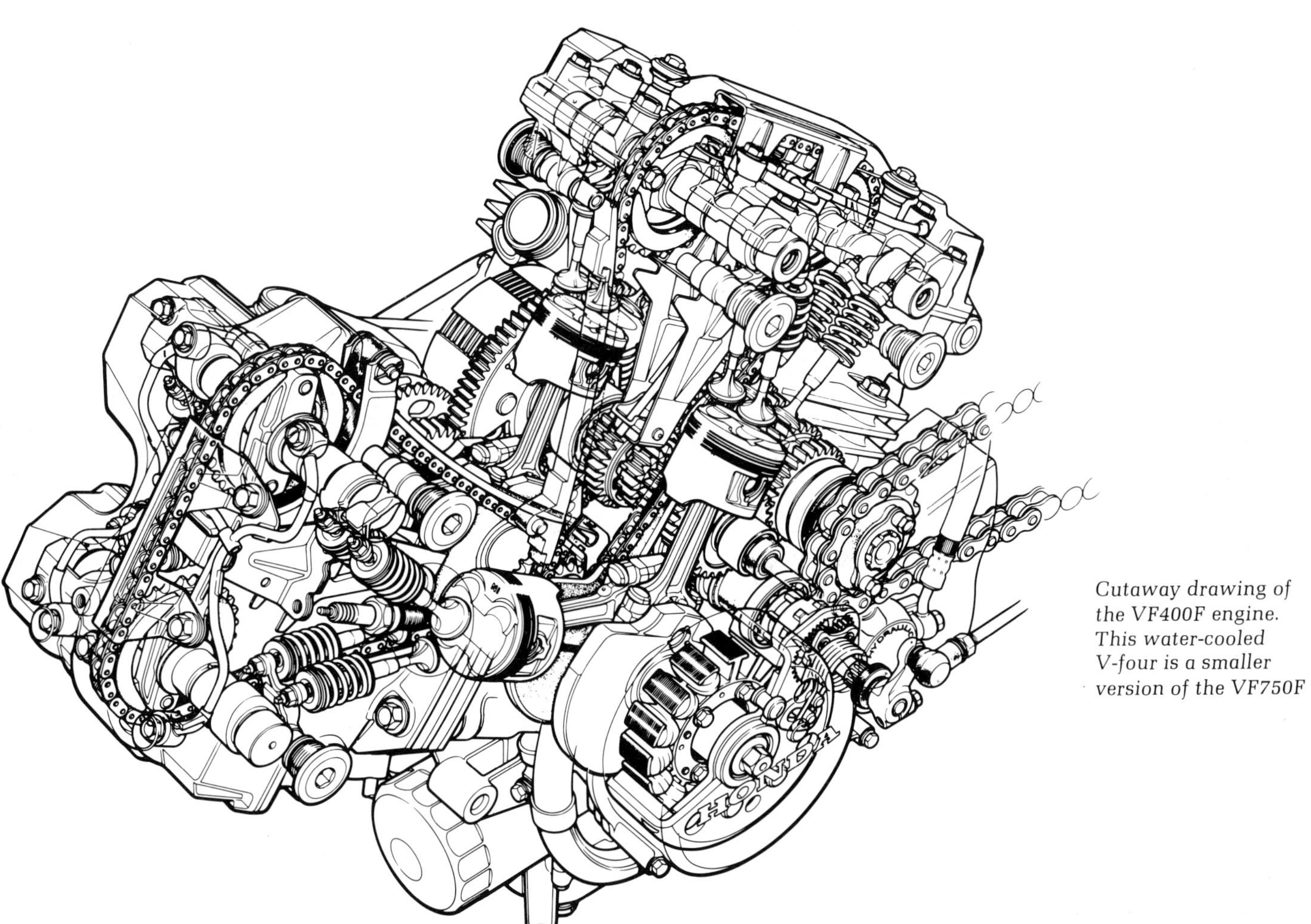

Cutaway drawing of the VF400F engine. This water-cooled V-four is a smaller version of the VF750F

11,500 rpm for this sophisticated eight-valve machine and with a well-braced cradle-type frame and single shock Pro Link suspension at the rear, handling is well up to power output. Sophisticated features like a maintenance-free hydraulic clutch and anti-dive front forks are unique for this size of bike.

Incredibly, Honda also launched a 250 cc two-stroke roadster – their first for decades. Restricted to Japan only at the time of writing, but it is selling 'like hot cakes', and no wonder for its engineering comes straight from the grands prix-winning NS500 triple! Known as the MVX250 and, like the NS500, it has a water-cooled two-stroke V3 engine with reed valve induction. There are differences: the racer has a 112 degree vee with one cylinder forward, whilst the two-fifty has a 90 degree configuration with two cylinders forward. The roadster is styled just like the racer, even down to the aluminimum silencers and has been reported capable of speeds up to 115 mph (184 kph). Frame and running gear are like the racer. In fact, apart from the physical difference in size, the machines are almost identical.

Heavyweights

The CB400N Super Dream has been revamped for the 1980s and uses a bored-out version of the 250N mill. Sold in Japan and the USA as the Hawk (in the US as a 450 cc), the 395 cc CB400 has the latest twin-piston front disc calipers for sure stopping, Comstar wheels, six-speed gearbox and counter balance shafts to iron out even those tiny little vibrations. The custom version – the CM400T – is not available in the UK.

The American version – the CB450T Hawk – uses the same engine bored out to 75 mm from 70.5 mm but has a number of other changes. There is only one front disc for example, while the handlebars are higher and the Comstar wheels are picked out in matt black. Also only available in the USA is the custom-styled CB450T Nighthawk.

Despite the fact that the CB400 twin was a more powerful machine than the late-lamented CB400F four it superseded, the later bike never really caught the public's imagination in the same way. For years now motor cyclists all over the world – especially in Britain – have been calling for Honda to produce a machine that captured the excitement of the CB400F . . . now they have it in the VF400F. This 120-mph (192-kph) V4 is an out and out sports machine that thrives on revs. It is fitted with an electronic cut-out that knocks off the revs when the 14,000 rpm limit is reached.

Maximum output is 53 bhp and that comes in way up at 11,500 rpm. Virtually a doubled-up VT250 (see Middleweights section), the VF400 is a 90 degree water-cooled V4 with double overhead camshafts, 16 valves and an hydraulic clutch. Tests have shown that the VF can turn in a 13 second quarter-mile . . . very very fast. Like the VT, the VF has a double loop cradle-type frame, Pro Link suspension and anti-dive forks.

Completely new for the 1980s is the very

FT500 Ascot (US specification)

CX500E Sports

GL500 Silver Wing Tourer (US specification)

CBX550F

CBX400F (Japanese specification)

CB650SC Nighthawk (US specification)

CB650 Custom
(Japanese specification)

exciting FT500 ohc four-stroke single-cylinder roadster, known as the Ascot in the USA. Very much a US-inspired bike, the FT500 is derived from the XR500-based machines campaigned on flat-track circuits in the United States. It has fat tyres (3.50 × 19 inches at front, 4.25 × 18 inches at rear), box-section swing arm and long-travel, leading-axle front forks. In keeping with flat-track traditions it also has single disc brakes front and rear – both with twin-piston calipers – and a two-into-one black competition-style exhaust on the right side.

The FT500's engine is a modified version of the four-valve, twin-exhaust port XR500 enduro mill but the bottom end is completely new and incorporates a counter rotating balancer shaft to reduce the big single's vibrations; it also has an electric starter. The FT gets a new 43 mm constant vacuum carburettor, too.

Most popular over 250 cc Hondas in Britain for many years is the trend-setting CX500 water-cooled V-twin. This machine with its novel engine layout, an across-the-frame 80 degree vee with four-valve cylinder heads operated by pushrods, plus the refinement of shaft-drive immediately appealed to long distance tourers and serious commuters alike who wanted fuss-free running. Lately Honda have boosted the capacity to 650 cc and added three more CX650 options: the CX650E Sports with single rear shock Pro Link suspension, Eurostyling and nose fairing; the GL650 Silver Wing Tourer with Pro Link, full fairing and removable rear luggage trunk; and of course *the* machine of the 1980s – the Honda CX650 Turbo (see Superbikes section).

Honda have come up with a real gem in their CBX550F four (introduced in 1982). This high performance machine is sure to re-establish the company in one area where they have not had a contender for several years – the 400 cc to 500 cc four-cylinder market.

The CBX550 has everything – double overhead cams, sixteen valves, six gears, transistorised contactless ignition ... and a novel braking system. Inboard ventilated discs are the stoppers on this innovative sportster. Honda have installed floating discs within a beautifully cast hub each gripped by one of the new twin-piston caliper brakes. There are twin discs at the front, one at the rear.

The engine (acually 572 cc with a bore and stroke of 59.2 × 55 mm) produces a claimed 62 bhp at 10,000 rpm. The CBX550 also has an oil cooler, Pro Link rear suspension, alloy rim Comstar wheels, and the TRAC (Torque-Reactive Anti-dive Control) anti-dive front suspension. Dry weight is claimed at 405 lb (184 kg).

Other variants of the 550 include an F2 version with a fairing and, in some European countries, a 400 cc version – the CBX400F with single front disc. This similarly-styled machine displaces 399 cc (55 × 42 mm bore and stroke) and produces 48 bhp at 11,000 rpm.

At the top of the middleweight class are the 650 cc Hondas – machines for big bike riders who want to save a little on running costs and insurance, but who do not want to skimp on performance, equipment or style.

The only CB650 four available in the UK at present is the CB650SC (known as the Nighthawk). The 650 uses the familiar 627 cc (59.855.8 mm) four-cylinder mill but it's fitted in a re-styled custom package. There are four-into-four magaphone-style exhaust pipes, a dual seat beautifully sculpted into a sort of 'low rise' King and Queen seat, while the tank is lined in chrome and the rear tyre is a fat 16-inch (40-cm) cover. Front suspension is the latest air-assisted leading axle type. Comstar wheels are picked out in black and the dual front disc brakes – twin-piston items – are supplemented by a single drum at the rear.

The other 650 cc Honda four currently available is the CB650 Custom that has a single front disc, and does without the new front forks, sculpted dual seat or luxury paint job. Like the SC machine, however, the standard Custom machine has the latest adjustable handlebars that can be altered by up to 30 mm vertically and 25 mm horizontally to suit individual tastes.

CB750F
(US specification)

VF750S

VF750 Magna
(US specification)

VF750F

The Superbikes

The first-ever 750 cc four was Honda's legendary CB750. When the machine was launched in 1969 it took the bike world by storm and the name 'superbike' was coined. The original sohc machine is no more, but the spirit lives on in the latest CB750F machine that has the benefits of over 10 years of CB750 development built in.

The latest 750 is the smaller brother of the world endurance championship-winning CB900 racer. The engine, as one would expect, is a dohc four with four valves per cylinder, electronic ignition, five speeds, electric start, triple disc brakes – now with dual pistons – 30-way adjustable rear FVQ dampers and taper-roller steering bearings.

The standard CB750F comes with four-into-two pipes but there is a custom version with four-into-four pipes, a 16-inch rear tyre, King and Queen seat, leading axle front forks and high, wide handlebars. In 1982 a three-quarter faired version – the CB750F2 – was also added to the range.

The sensation of the 1981 Milan Motor Cycle Show in Italy was the completely new VF750S Honda – the world's first production bike with a liquid-cooled V4. The bike was so innovative and different that it really proved Honda can do almost anything with a motor cycle.

Drawing from their experience with the NR500 V4 500 cc grand prix racer, Honda produced for the VF750 a 90 degree V4 with the crank sited across the frame. The bike is equipped with an hydraulic clutch, single-shock Pro Link suspension, double overhead camshafts, four valves per cylinder plus a whole host of other new features, including a system check display, gear indicator and an anti-theft device.

Honda claim a whopping 82 bhp (the CB750 produces 79 bhp) at 9,500 rpm from this 748 cc (70 × 48.6 mm) mill. Despite the refinements of shaft-drive and water-cooling the VF still only weighs 484 lb (219 kg) dry – 15 lb *less* than the CB750! Bank angle is an incredible 43 degrees and a modified engine in a race frame has shown great potential on the tracks.

A custom version – the VF750 Magna – is available in the USA. The Magna has leading-axle front forks with extra rake, a King and Queen seat, and to keep the appearance of the teardrop tank there is a small back-up reservoir – linked to the main tank, of course – situated under the seat. The Magna has remote reservoir rear shocks.

Based on the Daytona bikes, the latest V4 is the VF750F, the fastest non-turbocharged production seven-fifty in the world. The water-cooled machine is mechanically identical to the smaller VF400F (see Heavyweights section), but with a top speed of close-on 140 mph (224 kph) it is a little faster! It has been recorded as running the quarter-mile in 11.96 seconds.

The styling is designed to make the machine look much like the racers, with a box section tubular steel frame and top half fairing. Like the racers it has a 16-inch (41-cm) front wheel for quicker, more precise steering. Honda claim

CB900F2

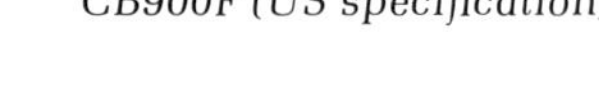

CB900F (US specification)

GL1100 De Luxe

CX500 Turbo (US specification)

90 bhp at 10,000 rpm for the VF750F, which is almost 30 bhp more than the first 750 cc four they produced – the CB750F of 1969.

Literally the road-going version of the 1979 World Endurance championship-winning racer, the CB900F really is a mover. Sharing a powerplant similar to the CB750, the nine-hundred has a power output of a whacking 91 bhp at 9,000 rpm and 130 mph (209 kph) can be got out of this superbike. An F2 version with three-quarter fairing is available, and in the USA Honda have the extraordinary CB900C Custom. Basically using the same engine, Honda have added a transfer box to CB900C that allows the rider to stop and choose between a high or low gear ratio. That means 10 gears in all and not surprisingly a slightly longer wheelbase. Transfer box apart, the Custom model has all the usual refinements like high handlebars and dual level seat.

The fastest-production bike Honda has produced so far is the 140-mph (224-kph) CB1100R superbike. It has been built only in limited quantities for racers who want to own the fastest thing on two wheels. The engine is based on the CB900F but bored from 64.5 mm to 70 × 69 mm (1,062 cc) and given hotter cams and other refinements that boost the available power from 91 to

120 bhp . . . that comes all in at 9,000 rpm.

In 1982 the 1100R got a new dual seat that converts to a single seat with the addition of a bumstop. Other new features included ventilated discs, dual-piston calipers, TRAC anti-dive front suspension on both fork legs, Michelin M48 tubeless tyres (front and rear), steel-braided brake hoses, a new air vent system to speed refuelling . . . indeed a whole host of detail improvements that make the CB1100R as much a winner on the race tracks as on the road.

Honda broke new ground when they launched the flat-four water-cooled Gold Wing grand tourer in the mid-1970s. The latest 1980s Gold Wing has an 1,100 cc engine and a whole host of detail improvements, including a sophisticated compressor system linked to the suspension so that the rider can select ride height *on the move*. For the serious touring rider adjustable ride height is a definite bonus as he can compensate for different loads, pillions, terrain, and so on.

The GL1100 De Luxe features electronically cancelling indicators, a full deluxe fairing with adjustable air vents and screen and ventilated disc brakes all round. The buyer of the standard model 'Wing has to do without the adjustable ride control and fairing, but he still gets a mean long-distance tourer that will enable him to cover hundreds of miles in a day and still arrive fresh.

Above: CB1100R

Below: XL500R

XL250R (Japanese specification)

XL125S (Japanese specification)

XL185S Super Farmer

However, the 'ultimate tourer' in the Honda range is the GL1100 Aspencade. The Aspencade has everything the De Luxe version has, but with a 'take-away' digital stereo radio, optional 40 channel CB rig and a stereo cassette deck! Remote controls for the CB and radio are mounted on the handlebars, while the instrumentation features digital readouts for the radio stations as well as engine monitors.

One of the mid-1980s sensations from the Honda stable is the CX650 Turbo (originally launched as the CX500 Turbo in 1981). This 650 machine sets new highs in technical sophistication: electronically-computerised fuel injection, a highly refined turbocharging system, digital instrumentation ... the CX650T is much, much more than a turbocharged CX650. In fact, the Turbo represents a whole new way of looking at the concept of superbikes.

The Turbo offers the performance of a nine-hundred and the light weight and economy of a five-hundred while the technical sophistication is revolutionary. It is in a class of its own – the world's first production turbocharged roadster.

The engine is a completely re-engineered CX650. The power output is way up to 90 bhp and new forged pistons, heavy duty clutch and crankshaft bearings are all designed to take the strain. Honda have given the Turbo high capacity cooling and lubrication systems, digital computerised fuel injection that is pre-programmed for engine starting, warm up and will even compensate for high altitude running! The transistorised ignition system responds to engine speed and boost pressure. The full fairing and screen integrates into one flowing line with the machine's seat and tank. The whole machine has been timed at over 130 mph (208 kph). At the front Honda have fitted their new Torque-Reactive Anti-Dive Control (TRAC) that uses the torque on the brake calipers to stiffen up the damping on braking. The bike that has everything even has a self-diagnostic capability ... that means that if the unlikely event of one part of the fuel injection/turbo system fails then the computer compensates!

Trail Bikes

Although Honda were set to launch two-stroke trail bikes in the mid-1980s, their name has been established by a range of superb four-strokes. The biggest is the XL500R that features a powerful 33 bhp four-valve, twin exhaust port ohc engine with a neat device linking the kick start to an exhaust valve lifter for fuss-free starting.

The big XL has an enduro-style front headlamp, 12-volt electrics, five gears and Pro Link single-shock rear suspension just like the moto cross machines. Other features include a double leading shoe front brake, a counter balance shaft that reduces vibration and enduro-style quick release rear wheel assemblies. Dry weight is 297 lb (135 kg).

The XL250R shares all of the five-hundred's features but only has a single leading shoe front brake. The 74 × 57.8 mm mill produces 22 bhp and a six-speed gearbox is fitted. Also in the range is the XL250S which is very similar to the R model, but does not have the Pro Link rear suspension. To provide for every ability and purse Honda also provide an XL100, XL125s and an XL185S . . . all sohc single-cylinder four-stroke trail irons.

One of the latest additions to Honda's trail range is the CL250S – a real luxury dual-purpose machine that is designed for really comfortable road riding as well as the odd backwoods jaunt. Using the same 250 cc ohc motor as the XL250, though a little detuned to produce just 20 bhp (as opposed to 22 bhp), the CL250 features a soft dual seat, electric starter and an extra low first gear.

It is not only those who venture off road for fun that Honda makes trail bikes for . . . they also do two machines specifically designed for farmers to get about their estates. The CT185 Super Farmer is an XL185-based farm bike with a fully enclosed chain case, handlebar guard levers, automatic decompressor, full knobbly tyres, clutch lever lock that allows you to leave the bike idling in gear, two side stands – one on either side – and a foot protector. The CT185 is aimed specifically at the Australian farmer – but a 125 cc version is also available in Europe.

For the off-road competitor – in moto cross or enduros – Honda cater for all capacity classes. There is also a full range of ATC (All Terrain Cycles) – three-wheelers designed for serious off road transport as well as fun.

The enduro competitors can choose from XR80, 100, 200, 350 and 500 cc mounts. All are single-cylinder four-strokes – all powerful and all competitive.

New for the 1980s is the highly-acclaimed XR200RC – smallest of the single rear-shock Pro Link machines that like its bigger brothers has a QD rear wheel, air-assisted front forks, and a countdown trip meter for those long distance events. The XR350R has a six-speed close ratio gearbox, and all the necessary enduro-bike features. The XR500, like the 250 and 500 cc XLs, has a counter rotating balancer shaft to iron out the bad vibrations.

For the moto cross competitor Honda have 80, 125, 250 and 480 cc mounts. Unlike the Enduros they are all two-strokes and the biggest machine, the CR480R, is a replica of the bike that Belgian André Malherbe won the 1981 World Moto Cross Championship on.

The CR480RC (actually 472 cc) is a real beastie: the big 38 mm carburettor and new porting arrangement gives a whacking 51 bhp. Like the works machines, the four-eighty has Pro Link rear suspension, electronic ignition, Pro Link rear suspension that can be externally adjusted and air-assisted front forks with huge 43 mm diameter stanchions for flex-free movement. The Pro Link has four compression damping adjustments, a more progressive spring action and the front brake is now a twin leading shoe design in magnesium alloy.

Honda's famous ATC three-wheeler range runs from the little ATC 70C (a four-stroke model), all

CT185 Super Farmer (Australian specification)

CT125

XR200 (US specification)

HONDA
500R
XR
PRO-LINK

the way up to the hairy two-stroke ATC 250R. All but the two-fifty have an automatic clutch for easy riding and the fat tyres have such a low contact pressure that they can go where even moto cross machines will get bogged down.

Farmers in the USA and Australia use machines like the ATC 185 for serious farm work, such as carrying loads on a trailer and checking out those outlying barns. There is an ATC to suit everyone – 70, 110, 185, 200 and 250 cc. The ATC 185 has a five-speed transmission, 12-volt electrics, recoil starter with automatic decompressor, and runs on big 11.8-inch (30-cm) wide, 22-inch (55.9-cm) diameter tyres.

One of the most recent developments is the two-stroke ATC 250R. Definitely just for fun and competition, this ATC has a five-speed gearbox, manual clutch, air suspension, and disc brakes. There is even a balance shaft to keep the vibrations down. The 250R has a big 60-watt headlamp, and all the other ATCs – with the sole exception of the 70 – have headlamps.

To complete the off-road picture, there is the tiny Z50R fun bike. Just the job for junior to find his way around on a motor cycle, the Z50R has an automatic clutch, three-speed transmission, moto cross looks and should turn any youngster on to the delights of motor cycling ... safely.

Opposite, top: *XR500R (US specification)*

Opposite, bottom: *this small ATC, the 70-B, was designed with youngsters in mind*

Above: *ATC 250R*

Honda's Achievements

1946 Honda technical research institute established in Hamamatsu by Soichiro Honda where auxiliary engines for bicycles and machine tools were produced.

1947 Kiyoshi Kawashima, who succeeded Soichiro Honda as president of the company in 1973, joined Honda.

1948 Honda Motor Company was established in Hamamatsu. By October the A-type engine (a 50 cc two-stroke) had gained a 66 per cent share of the domestic market. That month Honda's first true motor cycles, the 90 cc B-type was marketed.

1949 The first Honda motor cycle to carry the name Dream went on sale. This was the two-stroke 100 cc D-type machine.

1950 A second branch and manufacturing plant were set up in Tokyo.

1951 The first mass production four-stroke – the 146 cc Dream E-type – was launched on the domestic market. Production was 130 units a day, a record for the infant Japanese motor cycle manufacturers of the day.

1952 A third plant was set up at Shirako and the first machines were exported – to Taiwan, Okinawa and the Philippines. Production of engines for agricultural use was started.

1953 The Benly J-type 90 cc was launched and further factories opened at Saitama and Hamamatsu.

1954 Honda shares went public on the Tokyo Stock exchange. Honda machines participated in a race in Brazil – the factory's first international sporting venture. Soichiro Honda attended the Isle of Man TT races. The 140 cc Benly JA-type and 200 cc Juno Scooter went into production.

1955 Four new models were launched including the 250 cc and 350 cc Dreams. By the end of the year Honda were Japan's largest producers of motor cycles.

1956 Service division was established and one year guarantee system introduced.

1957 The factory racing team took the first five places in the junior class of the Mount Asami race. The C70 250 cc Dream was introduced.

1958 The step-through Super Cub C100 (50 cc) was launched – forerunner of the 70 cc and 90 cc step-through models which have sold in their millions around the world. The first model with electric starting, the 250 cc Dream C71 was marketed.

1959 The racing team competed for the first time in Europe – in the 125 cc Isle of Man TT. American Honda Motor Company was established.

1960 New head office building was completed in Tokyo and the Suzuka factory was opened. The stylish C72 250 cc Dream was introduced. The now famous R and D (Research and Development) Department was set up as a separate company and the sporting 250 cc CB72 was launched.

1961 The racing team achieved their first major successes by winning both the 125 cc and 250 cc Isle of Man TT races, both bikes being ridden by Mike Hailwood. The team went on to win the Manufacturers World Championships in both classes. The first European subsidiary, Honda Deutschland GmbH, was established in Hamburg. Overseas production was started in Taiwan and sales of machines around the world topped 100,000 a month – a record for a motor cycle manufacturer.

1962 Honda Benelux NV was established to assemble and sell motor cycles in Europe. Construction of the Suzuka circuit was completed. Honda continued their international racing successes by taking three Manufacturers World Championships – the 125 cc, 250 cc and 350 cc.

1963 An assembly plant in Belgium was completed and the Honda Foundry Company was set up in Japan together with a specialised parts division established to speed the flow of spare parts. Honda won the Manufacturers World Championship for the 250cc and 350 cc classes.

1964 Honda France was established in Paris and the company branched out into Formula 1 car racing as well as continuing to contest the motor cycle grands prix.

1965 Honda UK was set up in London. Honda won their first Formula 1 car race when Ritchie Ginther was successful in the Mexican Grand Prix. The CB450, their first mid-range machine, was launched.

1966 A factory was set up in Thailand. The company set a record by winning all five solo classes (50 cc, 125 cc, 250 cc, 350 cc and 500 cc) of the Manufacturers World Championship.

1967 Worldwide sales of the step-through Cub model topped the 5 million mark. The racing team again dominated the road racing grands prix, winning three (250 cc, 350 cc and 500 cc) Manufacturers World Championships.

1968 Just 20 years after starting to make motor cycles Honda's cumulative output topped 10 million machines.

1969 The first superbike, the four-cylinder CB750, was introduced. Motor cycle production topped 12 million. Honda Australia and Honda Canada were established.

1970 A race-kitted CB750 won the Daytona 200 race in America – the first Japanese machine to do so. The first three-wheeler ATC model was launched. Exports of motor cycles topped 5 million. Honda gave the American YMCA 10,000 mini-bikes as part of a drive to stop delinquency.

1971 Production of motor cycles started in Mexico and a subsidiary was opened in Brazil. The first medium capacity four-cylinder model (the CB500) was developed for launching the following year.

1972 The company moved into the moto cross market with the two-stroke CR250M machine and launched the first small capacity four-cylinder four-stroke, the CB350F. A five-day week was introduced at all the Japanese factories.

1973 Kiyoshi Kawashima took over as President of the company upon the retirement of Soichiro Honda and Vice President Takeo Fujisawa. Distributors from 37 countries travelled to Japan to celebrate the company's 25th anniversary.

1974 The luxury Gold Wing GL1000 and four-cylinder CB400F were marketed. Subsidiaries were established in Switzerland and Peru.

1975 Output and sales affected by slump in American market with annual output slipping from the record 2,132,902 of the previous year to 1,782,448.

1976 Honda officially entered the FIM endurance series and won the two most prestigious awards – the overall championship and the French 24-hour *Bol d'Or*.

1977 President Kiyoshi Kawashima startled the sporting world when he announced that they were to return to World Championship grand prix racing with a 500 cc four-stroke. The statement was made to foreign journalists in Japan for the launch of their supreme superbike – the six-cylinder CBX1000.

1978 Motor cycle production for the year rocketed to a record 2,639,738 units.

1979 Entry into moto cross racing was crowned with the highest award when Graham Noyce of England won the 500 cc World Championship.

1980 Motor cycle production for the year topped 3 million for the first time. The actual output for the year from the Japanese-based Honda factories was 3,087,471 – over 11,000 every working day! Factory rider André Malherbe of Belgium took over as 500 cc Moto Cross World Champion.

1981 The company beat the opposition to market the first production machine fitted with a turbocharger – the V-twin, water-cooled CX500 Turbo. Malherbe retained his Moto Cross World Championship.

1982 American Freddie Spencer scored Honda's first 500 cc road racing grand prix win since 1967 when he won the Belgian Grand Prix on the new two-stroke, three-cylinder NS500 in July.

1983 Capitalising on the success of the NS500 road racer Honda launched a sports three-cylinder 250 cc roadster – the factory's first high performance road-going two-stroke.

Index

Acknowledgements

Many of the illustrations in this book have been supplied by Honda and *Motor Cycle Weekly*; for additional material the publishers are grateful to: John Dickinson; Wolfgang Gruber; N. Haskell; Jan Heese; S. Mallinson; David Maltais; Don Morley; Chris Myers; B. R. Nicholls; Mick Woollett; and Leo Vogelzang